DIANE TESSMAN HA
HER ACCOUNT OF CH
INTER-DIMENSION
VERIFIED BY SEVERA

MW00936922

RUTH MONTGOMERY HAS THIS TO SAY:

"I asked the Guides for any further comment on Diane's channeling. They replied, 'Diane's contacts are real. It should be stressed that Space People are indeed able to contact through mental telepathy those who are open to their vibrations....'"

Excerpt from ALIENS AMONG US by Ruth Montgomery
Published by P.G. Putman's Sons

DR. LEO SPRINKLE STATES:

"In 1981, Diane and her daughter came to Laramie so that Diane might explore, through hypnotic procedures, her memories of her UFO experiences. My own interpretation of the reactions by Diane to the hypnotic procedures was as follows: Diane's reactions were vivid in recall, or memories, of real experiences which have a profound influence on her inner character and her personal goals. In other words, these memories were of 'real experience' as far as Diane is concerned. Does that mean that the information obtained through channeling from Tibus by Diane is true? I do not know. Perhaps time will tell us the answers to that question."

Psychologist and Professor of Counseling Services
University of Wyoming

1

DIANE TESSMAN

Cover art by Carlos Ramos

All photos taken by Timothy Green Beckley and Della Van Hise

The first printing of THE TRANSFORMATION (ISBN 0-938294-59-8) was Published by: INNER LIGHT PUBLICATIONS P.O. Box 753 New Brunswick, N.J. 08903.

This edition published by Diane Tessman at P.O. Box 352, Ansgar, Iowa, 50472. Website is at http://earthchangepredictions.com and her email address is info@earthchangepredictions.com. Kindle book version published on March 6, 2014. CreateSpace edition published in March 2014. Manuscript prepared by Mark A. Valco.

Table of Contents

Here I am with Dr. Sprinkle in his office at the University of
Wyoming just after our hypnosis session.

THE UNIVERSITY OF WYOMING
COUNSELING CENTER
344 KNIGHT HALL TELEPHONE 766-2187
LARAMIE, WYOMING 82071

INTRODUCTION

Dear Reader:

I am pleased and honored to introduce you to the writer: Ms.

4

Diane M. Tessman. I wish to offer you some information about this person from whom you will gain much knowledge.

My initial (conscious) reaction to Ms. Tessman was one of doubt. I opened her June, 1980 letter which described her interest in UFO investigations, and saw a photograph which she had included in order to remind me that we had met earlier at a UFO conference. I told my secretary that I would have remembered anyone who was as attractive as the person in that photograph!

As I continued to read the letter from Ms. Tessman, I gained another impression - the writer is bright, educated, and shows an objective and scientific orientation toward the problems of UFO research.

As we corresponded further, and as she described her experiences and her investigations of UFO sightings and related psychic events, I formed another impression - Ms. Tessman shows the characteristics of a good UFO investigator, including curiosity, courage, and compassion.

I somehow sensed, in viewing a photograph of her group of elementary school pupils, that she is a teacher in the true sense of the title: someone who shares of herself so that the learner can gain self-knowledge as well as knowledge about the outside world.

But Diane Tessman is more than a UFO investigator, and more than an elementary school teacher; she also is a UFO contactee. She receives information from intelligent beings who claim to be extraterrestrial in origin and benign in purpose. Do we know this claim to be true? We do not. Do we know if Diane is accurate in her description of her experiences and in her interpretation of their significance? Perhaps each reader must answer that question on the basis of personal experience - or on the basis of personal belief, bias, and prejudice.

For me, it was a simple task to determine my own reaction to Diane's claims. I asked her to participate in a "survey of psychic impressions of UFO phenomena." I have been investigating claims of UFO observers for over 21 years. Long ago, I decided to emphasize the exploration, rather than the evaluation, of individual claims of UFO contactees. (My hope is that the exploration of individual claims will lead investigators, someday, to analysis and understanding of the patterns of UFO experiences and their possible scientific and social significance.)

My own UFO experiences, and my own investigations of UFO abductees and contactees, had caused me to shift my initial viewpoint of "scoffer" to "skeptic" to "believer" that UFO phenomena are real, both physically and psychically. (Theoretical physicists describe the dilemma of light, which can be viewed as "particle" and "wave"; UFO researchers recognize the dilemma of UFOs, which can be described as "spacecraft" and "psychic phenomena.") I accept the hypothesis that I am both "investigator" and "contactee" in the UFO network; both "particle" and "wave" in the "light" of UFO activity.

Thus, Dear Reader, please be aware of my favorable bias toward the acceptance of various "levels of reality" of UFO phenomena. But, also, Dear Reader, please recognize that my bias is not merely prejudice: I have expended personal energy, money, and time in an effort to explore and to understand the world view of the UFO contactee.

Since 1965,1 have obtained completed questionnaires and psychological profiles from several hundred UFO contactees. Thus, my response to the claims of Diane Tessman was to ask her to participate in this survey. Diane was willing to complete the survey materials, which included a questionnaire on her background and her ESP and UFO experiences, and the psychological inventories: Vocational Preference Inventory (VPI), 16 Personality Factors Test (16PF), and the Minnesota Multiphasic Personality Inventory (MMPI).

The pattern of profile scores indicated, according to my interpretation, that Diane's scores were similar to those scores of USA females who are high in abstract intelligence and who are viewed as self-sufficient; there was no indication of neurotic or psychotic reactions; there was a pattern of high interests in intellectual, realistic, and artistic, activities, but little interest in status or social prestige; there was a pattern of "normal" personality characteristics, with a tendency toward feminine interests, a tendency toward shyness in social situations, and an indication of high "ego-strength" or the ability to deal with difficult emotional situations. In summary, the profile scores showed a pattern of "normal" responses, indicating that Diane had responded like those persons who are viewed as self-sufficient, emotionally spontaneous, somewhat socially reserved, and who have high interests in scientific, intellectual, and artistic activities.

Diane's questionnaire responses were similar to those of many other participants in the survey: descriptions of her UFO observations (in 1966,1979, and 1980), with comments which indicated that she had checked on her current aeronautical and meteorological conditions as possible explanations for her UFO sightings. Her responses to questions about UFOLKS, or UFO occupants, showed that she was familiar with the various hypotheses about UFO encounters and the possible explanations for the (alleged) UFOLKS. Also, she showed an awareness of her own development as a UFO witness/ investigator/contactee.

In 1981, Diane and her daughter, Gianna, came to Laramie with Dottie Burrow of Denver, Colorado, so that Diane might explore, through hypnotic procedures, her memories of her UFO experiences. On August 13, 1981, Diane responded to my questions and suggestions so that we could obtain subconscious impressions of her encounters and communications with UFOLKS.

I have worked with approximately 150 persons who have described in hypnosis sessions their memories (or impressions) of their UFO encounters and abductions by UFOLKS. I am impressed by the sincerity and fortitude of these persons, as they sometimes describe painful and frightening reactions to their experiences. However, it was a pleasure to work with Diane. Her level of intelligence, her level of knowledge, and her level of self-awareness allowed her to minimize her doubts and fears, and to maximize the exploration of the significance and meaning of her memories and impressions.

My own interpretation of the reactions by Diane to the hypnotic procedures was as follows: Diane's reactions were vivid recall, or memories, of real experiences which have a profound influence on her inner character and her personal goals. In other words, these memories were of "real" experiences as far as Diane is concerned. Does that mean that the information obtained by Diane is true? I do not know. Perhaps time will tell us the answers to that question.

The Who, Where, When, What, How, and Why of UFO experiences is a puzzle. However, if these bizarre, baffling, and sometimes bothersome events continue, then more and more persons will find themselves involved. They may find themselves going through the doubt, depression, and difficulty of understanding what they perceived; where their world view changed; when they noticed the metamorphosis; what their life purpose or task may be; how they can accomplish their mission; and of course, "Why Me?" They may find themselves going through various levels (stages of development?) of UFO experiences.

A MODEL OF THE TIME, RANGE, AND LEVEL OF UFO EXPERIENCES
TENTATIVE DEFINITION OF TERMS

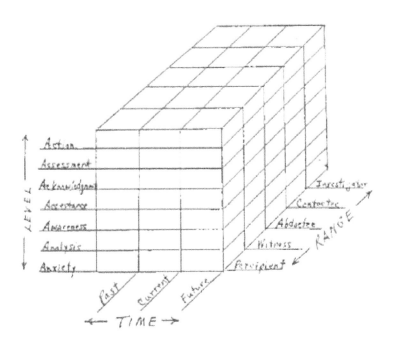

I.   TIME OF UFO EXPERIENCES:
      Past   Categories of "time" could be in
      Current terms of days, months, years,
      Future   lifetimes, civilizations, etc.

II.   RANGE OF UFO EXPERIENCES:
      Percipient: One who perceives/intuits the matter/energy of

9

UFO phenomena.

Witness: One who informs one or more other persons of his/her UFO experience(s).

Abductee: One who is physically and/or psychically (OBE*) taken aboard a UFO.

Contactee: One who communicates with and/or receives information from UFOLKS (UFO occupants).

Researcher: One who searches for UFO evidence; analyzes information; and/or shares information about UFO experiences with others.

*OBE: Out-of-body experience; i.e., "body" in one space location and "mind" in another location.

III.   LEVEL OF UFO EXPERIENCES:

Anxiety: A feeling (which can be mild doubt, some dread, or deep despair) that "something is wrong" which was held by the UFO percipient prior to his/her UFO experience(s).

Analysis: An attempt by the UFO percipient to gain understanding, to rationalize, or to explain the significance and meaning of the UFO experience(s).

Awareness: Recognition by the UFO percipient that she/he has experienced some kind of contact/encounter/communication with beings of "higher than human intelligence."

Acceptance: Recognition and resolution that the UFO experience occurred, despite the inner doubts of the UFO percipient and external criti cisms of others around the UFO percipient.

Acknowledgement: Recognition and resolution that the UFO percipient must respond to the reality of the UFO experience(s) by public declaration and/or by personal commitment to an appropriate life style or by goals(s) in life.**Assessment:** Re-evaluation by the UFO percipient of his/her lifestyle, physiological, in order to determine the physiological, and spiritual "costs" of completing the duty/goal/mission/task which is involved in his/her UFO connections.

Action: Activities, behaviors, commitments, and decisions which are oriented toward the completion of the duty/goal/mission/task of the UFO percipient.

(NOTE: An individual investigator or contactee could "plot" his/her UFO connections by noting the time, range, and level of

UFO experiences; for example, many contactees talk in terms of "past" and "future" lives; often they view their task as assisting others to change from "planetary persons" to "cosmic citizens.")

The model of UFO experiences (presented above) may have merit in conceptualizing the individuality or the "psychology" of the UFO experience. But what about the "sociology" of the UFO experience? What are the social manifestations and consequences? Unfortunately, we do not know, at this point, the effects of UFO activity on the economics, military, and political institutions of Earth's civilization. In fact, the governments of most nations seem to be hiding evidence about UFO activity.

If UFO experiences are contacts with highly developed intelligent beings, then we must assume that "they" have some goals or purposes in initiating, maintaining, and developing these contacts. Indeed, we are told by contactees that there are many specific purposes for each UFO experience, which "push" the contactee along his/her soul's journey by cleansing "past life" difficulties and preparing for "future life" developments. Also, we are told that there are two general goals of UFO activity:

　　　　(1)　To rejuvenate the Earth;
　　　　(2)　To assist Humankind in its evolutionary
　　　　development.

Some UFO contactees are told to prepare for possible cataclysms (Earth
changes, such as earthquakes, volcanic activity, etc.); some contactees are told to prepare for social, economic changes (possible nuclear war; possible collapse of governmental structure; etc.); some are told to prepare for spiritual changes (to become "teachers" and "healers" for the metamorphosis of humans into a "New Age" of science and spirituality, of high technology and high morality, of reason and religion). Usually, contactees are given messages which are "slightly misleading," which have caused some "objective" and "scientific" persons to reject the message - and the messenger!

Now, it seems that we can begin to ease our rejecting comments and to ask more meaningful questions of contactees: Which of these scenarios is "chosen" by a majority of contactees? Can humans use meditation and mediation to modify the possible destructive scenarios and to enhance the possible constructive scenarios? What do we have to "give up" in order to enter the

"New Age?"

Perhaps, in another generation, we will know which of the various scenarios - and which of the various responses - is the "real" and "right" reaction. Meanwhile, we can ponder over the various questions about UFO contactee experiences. Also, we can puzzle over the meaning of Diane's observations, encounters and contacts: How do her experiences compare with other UFO investigators and other UFO contactees? What advantages (and/or disadvantages) does she gain by public acknowledgement of her UFO experiences? Why is she being guided (or Nagged?! ?) into a more active role as contactee and investigator?

And now, Dear Reader, allow me to end my comments about Ms. Diane Tessman, and to turn my attention to you. What do you expect to learn by reading this book? When did you (or when will you permit yourself to) become aware of your own connections with UFO phenomena? How do you hope to deal with your own UFO connections? Where have you placed your favorite faith (or fear) about the New Age? Why have you (or why have you not) committed yourself to the realization of the New Age of science and spirituality, of psychic technology and scientific morality, of reason and religion?

I hope that your reading of this book brings to you renewed hope and faith in your own personal awareness and you own individual significance, as well as more information and knowledge about the growing network of UFO contactees and investigators.

May we all gain more Love and Light to illuminate our paths and to enlighten our lives.

R. Leo Sprinkle

1

THERE IS A MEANING TO

YOUR SEARCH

If you are reading this book, you have the need to search for something more.

If you are reading this book, you have urgent feelings that vast Earth changes will occur soon. The Creator Spirit has touched your soul in a very real way, either in childhood, recently, or throughout your life. Often you feel alienated and different from people around you who seem so oblivious to the final days of this planet, so uncaring about soul development and nourishment, so shallow and materialistic.

"But, I'm so confused..," you might say to yourself.

"Just where do I belong," and "What should I be doing to make this a better world?"

Often we find that we are walking a tightrope between functioning in this world and knowing with all our hearts that the time of great destruction is very near at hand. It is hard to be normal and act as if all will remain the same when your soul cries out for the time of transformation. Through crystal clear eyes, you see the petty materialism of this place, you see people hurting other people, stepping on them to get ahead, and you see the preoccupation with money, drugs, sex, shallow materialism, and you are sad. You see how little time most people spend in making their souls harmonious with the Cosmic Force of God, how cruel they are to Nature, to each other, and even to themselves. You see how quick they are to condemn one who is "different," and sometimes you feel great anger.

Perhaps concerned acquaintances have tried to use Freudian psychology to analyze your devotion to the enrichment of the soul, to Nature, to the knowledge that our Space Brothers and Sisters are out there, and to the Cosmic Force of God. Whether we are called contactees, UFO buffs, Jesus freaks, or psychic gurus, society makes fun of us who gently, quietly, and confidently know that there is more to the cosmos than this place and time.

"But," you might think, "sometimes I'm tempted to take part in things that are of this physical realm we live in."

And, of course, you should never feel guilty, for guilt is a cross we need not carry when we discover the true workings of the universe. Certainly, it is tempting to go bar hopping, to join socially with others, to get involved in more worldly activities because in this way we do not feel so alienated. However, we always revert back to seeing through crystal clear eyes, the shallowness, the lack of spiritual nourishment, the cruelty, and the ignorance. As the Change Times approach we return to our longing for the stars, our study of the Spirit and philosophy, and the development of our soul.

Why is it that we walk to a different drummer? Why do we look up to the stars at night in wonder and awe? Why do we listen to the pleading of our souls? Why do we crave more than this life can give us? And why do we know for certain that we are living in the "Last Days" - days of great disasters, changes and transformations?

I know, friend and reader, that you are one of us. I know that your soul is hurting and that this life has caused you great pain. I also know that your soul is a beautiful entity, like a flower in full bloom. But, still, you long for more. You long to sail the starry seas once more. You long to be transformed to a higher reality, to be good and kind and have great meaning to your existence without being made to compromise by the mundane world around you.

Your soul does not receive nourishment from the trivia on television, from meaningless jobs or social scenes, nor from the latest fad, and not even from earning money, the "god" of this place. In fact, money itself is not important to you; you do not care to keep up with the Jones'. You worry because of financial difficulties, but only in that you want to provide decently for your loved ones - and you do wish that you had more free time to devote to meditation, to being close to nature and to helping other humans and life forms.

"My God! I thought I was all alone."

Well, don't feel that way. There are others, many others, of us out here! How empty our lives would be if we did not look up at the stars and feel that bond that exists with Space Intelligence, with life throughout the universe, and with God.

How empty our lives would be if we did not dream dreams, if we did not have psychic insight, and if our souls did not cry out for spiritual nourishment! We would be as shriveled as dried out plants, not able to stretch, not searching, not growing, not surviving. Yes, we are the survivors. We will survive what is to come. We have the power, the will, to survive, and we have friends from Higher Realms to help us.

Many of us know that the "End Days" are coming and so we search the heavens for a higher meaning. Many of us are really ancient souls, and therefore we have had the opportunity to learn from mistakes made in previous lives. In our parallel aspects (past lives) we have had many trials, heartaches, as well as having known inner joys and pure peace. We have evolved to the level of consciousness which tells us that the cosmos is vast beyond comprehension, diverse beyond our wildest imagination, and that Higher Realms can be reached...not in fantasy, but in reality.

When we are regressed to past lives, we remember living in ancient times and many of us also remember parallel lives on far distant worlds. On Earth, we have been burned at the stake for our "powers" and beliefs. We have been exiled, tortured, imprisoned and crucified. Our souls survive and live in these bodies even now...and our souls will continue to survive long after these bodies perish in the cataclysm to come. It is true, however, that some of us will be "beamed up" to starships and will retain the bodies we have now; others of us will "die," only to move on to Higher Planes. But be warned! The powers that will be unleashed have the capacity to rip souls and the energy that comprises them to shreds.

And so, to the "Star Children" among us, to the seekers of "higher orders," to those who believe in miracles and prophecies, and to those searchers for cosmic enlightenment, this book is dedicated. It is dedicated to those who feel as I do-that we shouldn't give up. There are days when all seems so futile, when things seem stacked against us. But don't despair, for there is hope for those of us who dare to dream, to believe, to have faith. For we are the hope of the future, for we are the survivors of the great destruction. Remember that your spirit will still be alive and flourishing as a beautiful flower. We will no longer be "different," but we who have had the faith to believe will find our souls nourished in a beautiful new dimension.

THE SPACE BROTHER KNOWN AS TIBUS

Some of you may be confused by the statement on the cover of this book that some of the material contained within these pages was channeled through me by Tibus.

Tibus is a member of the Free Federation of Planets and has visited Earth many times. He is not as popular a Space Brother to channel as Ashtar or Monka. As far as I know, he channels only through me. At times, he commands a UFO (starship) and he is a good, highly evolved being. He has been my special contact since early childhood and ours is a rather unique case due to the quality and quantity of his channeled messages to me and to thousands of others.

However, this is not my book nor his book, but YOUR book! Through me, he has been given the assignment of laying out a survival guide to the End Days and subsequent Transformation, as well as to the stressful times which precede this period. Basically, what he wants is for you to hold on and be as strong as possible. I believe that if you follow the guideline offered in this book, your chances of survival will improve tenfold.

As for myself, I am a school teacher by profession, having taught eleven years in elementary school as well as English as a Second Language field, working with refugee children. For the past five years, I have offered spiritual guidance, given past life readings, and have done star person counseling for thousands of friends and clients. This shall continue to be my work until the coming Change Point.

As for my place of birth, I was born and raised in Iowa where my space contacts first took place. I've also lived in the Virgin Islands, and in Florida. In 1982,1 moved to sunny Poway, California, where I now devote full time to our star people's Starlight Center (non-profit) .But even with all that stretches out before me I ache for the day when the transformation begins and I can go home to my starry seas.

Diane Tessman and Tibus

2

MY SPECIAL ONE
TRANSCRIPT OF ACTUAL HYPNOTIC RECALL WITH DR. R. LEO SPRINKLE

On August 11,1981, Dr. R. Leo Sprinkle of the University of Wyoming placed me into an altered state of consciousness. At approximately 1:00 P.M., he gave me the suggestion that I should relax and began mental preparation for recall. He asked what level I was on on the "Hypnotical Yardstick," using the number 36 as the deepest hypnotic state possible. I responded that I was at level 20, but as the hypnotic state deepened, I reported being at level 28.

The following is Dr. Sprinkle's official log of my hypnotic session with him. The session began when he requested that I recall my earliest UFO experience.

Time: 1:15

Diane: I'm playing with Pat, my dog, on the farm. And I had stayed out late and Mom is inside cooking. Father's inside. I don't know where my brother is. The stars are clear, it is chilly, November. I am seven years old. And I have contact with something that has contacted me before, but I'm not allowed to remember. I want very much to remember them, though, and I try very hard. But this night, I worry about Pat, my dog, when I go with them. They say he is all right. (Pause)

And there is someone on board I know in particular, and I've known him each time. I'm not scared and I'm special, as other people are, but that to function in this life, in the mundane part of life that is ahead of me, that as protection, I cannot know the other side of me for a while, nor remember all that has happened. I love my mother and father, but every time I see them, I feel that this is where I belong. I always hate to leave. I always want to remember, but at that point...it is not allowed. (Pause)

I think that - they look like - fairly much like humans. I think that I've seen others on board who are not human, but they don't scare me. The one I know best is human and I love him. There is -

something - between us. He reassures that if they do something to me that is frightening or medical, that it is unimportant to me; I won't remember it and there is no suffering for it. He indicates that he has gone through something and he is okay. (Pause)

Time: 1:30

They - the different people on board, the different beings - all function smoothly together, and with love. I'm impressed there is no distinction between species. Then I go back to where my parents are and it's so ridiculous that people make distinctions between members of the human race.

I know that I will be watched - or monitored - throughout my life, until the point comes where I finally enter the world where I belong, where they are. I'm reassured. (Pause)

I think I'm shown a holograph - starfields-I don't know if I was really out in space but the Special One always showed me realistic holograms or space vistas. I loved to see them.

I feel that I am protected psychically. I can send out psychic messages easily when I want, but I am protected from receiving negative or false psychic messages until the time comes when all my psychic abilities must be opened up to insure survival.

I am remembering that right after that November night, whenever I laid down at night, they were able to monitor my thoughts with a mechanical device. NOT telepathy. They had to be close by to do this, a few miles away, and it annoyed me each night. My Special One wasn't there on these monitoring nights. It was two of them - just for a few minutes at a time.

I knew that he would be gone sometimes, far away, but I remember knowing that...or being told by him...that he and I were like on an experimental mission. Not a common thing... that he and I were doing. A sharing of self. I remember sadness for him.

(Comment by Dr. Sprinkle: At this point, Diane broke into silent tears. These tears lasted throughout the hypnosis sessions, a well of tears which seemingly would not stop...silent tears...which were felt from the very core of her being, from her soul itself, as these memories were received for the first time). I wanted to help him. He said I was. He said that all this was necessary, that he knew what he was doing, that he had freely consented to it. Whatever it was, it was harder on him than me. Suspension of life

18

as he knew it...a sacrifice. I felt that I was -1 hated it in his behalf - 1 felt my brain and age limited me; I couldn't fully understand it. And yet, in essence, I did understand it.
Time: 1:40

Slowly with the years, he knew that it would come together for me, as the time drew nearer. (Pause)

I remember, when I go for long walks on the farm, I go to several favorite hiding spots...and once in a while, he would appear in one of them, too. I think that's one reason I always went by myself to the creek - hoping that I would see... (long pause).

I remember the difference in the looks of the people in this world and the people on the ship. The people and beings on board seemed to blend physical abilities and good health with psychic abilities. They were advanced from humans. I have this distinct knowledge or impression that they were from the future Earth, at least the ones that look human -1 mean, the future earth after the turmoil and disaster and nuclear devastation. I think these people could look into this point in time and help us whenever they wished to do so. Some of the beings on board were definitely not from Earth, though, but they were gentle and highly intelligent. I don't know why my Special One - had to do something that would alter his path, which was so exciting and so beautiful.

Time: 1:45

I feel that he had someone special that I didn't know, who was strong and was overseeing the experiments, so that he would ultimately not be hurt by them.

(Comment by Dr. Sprinkle: Diane weeps harder as she describes her feelings that her Special One is not in a position to control, that someone else - a friend - is controlling the experiment; however, she is not sure why it was done - perhaps it is merely the assignment or mission or for our knowledge.)

I feel like I remember seeing the inside of the ship. I remember seeing the outside, too, of the small ship that picked me up. No, of a much, much larger ship. All I remember of the small ship that would pick me up was seeing lights in the night sky, then somehow being on board with them. But this big, big, ship was something so magnificent and powerful, it was like a dream. But inside, I'm in a corridor. There are many different rooms...circular. Some rooms have plants and rocks, that was the favorite room...the one that was like a forest. There are even nice animals. Other parts of the ship...it is so big, so very big...there is machinery and technical stuff and flashing lights that I was not allowed to touch.

I remember seeing him behind a translucent black screen in a room. It was a divided room...and he was standing behind this screen. I was being made to leave. I had to go. I knew I wouldn't see him again. I felt like I was being ripped away. In a way I felt as if he was coming with me.

(Comment by Dr. Sprinkle: Diane continues to cry as she is asked to tell of any further impressions.)

Time: 2:00

The large ship had a big view screen, wrap around. You could go and look out...(changing the subject): I keep thinking, if I had some of him, what was left of him? And I don't know. If I could, I would give it back to him, but it must be all right, that isn't the way...(Pause).

(Note: At this point Diane is asked to recall the exact date of the encounter. She comes up with November 7th.)

Dr. Sprinkle: Did you notice any strange behavior in Pat right before the encounter?

Diane: No.

Dr. Sprinkle: How did you get to the space ship?

Diane: I don't think it landed. It was hovering...the small ship that is. I feel that, one minute I was with Pat, the next I was gone. I was worried about him. I wondered what he thought...because all of me went on the ship, it was not an astral journey. I was on the ground one minute...and in the ship the next. The inside of the small ship - I'll call it a shuttle - was circular and it was too small for me to really feel comfortable. He - my Special One - is not on it this time. It's dull lighting - not misty, but it has a different look to it. Maybe the lights are low...not up at full strength. I think they are built into the ceiling, I can't see the specific source.

Dr. Sprinkle: The temperature?

Diane: I was cool, must have been cool, because I remember not being hot even with my jacket on.
Dr. Sprinkle: How were you dressed?

Diane: I had old corduroy pants...tennis shoes.

Dr. Sprinkle: What were the sounds on board?

Diane: There was this constant muted hum, almost musical and soft. I think there were computer hums and dings.

Dr. Sprinkle: Was there conversation?

Diane: I don't - there's no conversation, except with my Special One, but he isn't on the shuttle. I felt that I was going toward the bigger ship. I knew I wasn't to bother him on this trip. There were one or two small beings on the shuttle ship and they were busy.

Dr. Sprinkle: Were they human-like?

Diane: One was and one wasn't. It was more insect-looking, humanoid build, large eyes. I felt I wasn't supposed to memorize the...it was interesting, but unimportant to me. I wasn't supposed to observe too closely. I don't like this ship, it's squashed in - just a few feet of space.

Dr. Sprinkle: What are some of the features of the large ship?

Diane: It is so overwhelming. I love the places where you can see outside. And there are lots of trees, large plants, animals, and things that are familiar to me in this one area. I realize that people on board must love them as much as I love them - rocks, trees, animals - a vital part of the ship. There's a dome near the top and you can go up near the top of it and look out at the stars. The stars are vivid, not pinpoints like on earth, but actual balls of glowing light. I know somehow that the big ship could set its course and reach any one of these balls of light.

But for him - My Special One - Earth is home.

I felt that he was - no rank or military protocol on the ship - but he was loved, respected, one of the best.

Dr. Sprinkle: Are you sad to think of his life?

Diane: Sad, but also envious (weeping). I felt I should have been

included.

Dr. Sprinkle: What did he wear?

Diane: Plain, comfortable black. Sometimes it would vary. I think I might have seen him in blue jeans or Earth clothes, another time, a jumpsuit...pretty colors...sand-colored and black.

Dr. Sprinkle: Did he have insignia?

Diane: Very small...a black something...a black circle covered with a gold aerodynamic shape. Almost boomerang shaped.

Dr. Sprinkle: Was it a patch?

Diane: I don't know, I didn't question it. I was concerned with him - like, I could go back to my house, but I wouldn't look at the company name on my refrigerator. Pm not a "details" person.
Time: 2:20

Dr. Sprinkle: Did he have a belt and shoes?

Diane: Smooth, comfortable black shoes or boots.

Dr. Sprinkle: Was there conversation between you?

Diane: I think we experienced telepathy, but also talked verbally. It was like a teacher/student relationship, looking at the room of plants and animals, and him giving me some of his knowledge.

Dr. Sprinkle: Was there conversation between him and other crew members?

Diane: Yes, it was verbal, but I didn't understand it - whether it was technical or another language. I don't know. I don't think it was English. There was a room for contemplation that he took me to once, but he got interrupted there by crew-members asking things. He was always different with me, though. With them, he would be more official and harsh. I felt distant from the others, but I was his close friend. I was almost scared - he was so much beyond me.

Dr. Sprinkle: What about the ship's machinery?

Diane: The starship must have had hundreds of different departments or rooms. It was so much. I didn't understand it all. Not much stood out to me except the rocks and trees, yet I felt at home there. I didn't understand it all, but that fact didn't make me feel alienated.

I remember I saw a crystal or pane of glass. It looked like a dimension more than just glass - it was rectangular, as tall as me, with a rainbow of colors. I would look at it when I didn't have anything else to do. I don't know if it had a function or if it was just to look at. I saw some familiar things...medical equipment. I saw the medical area, but I can't remember it.

Dr. Sprinkle: Have you visited there?

Diane: He's with me when I go there. The doctor doesn't talk to me, but he's human. Possibly they took readings that were painless. Maybe some painful tests...I don't remember.

Time: 2:30

Dr. Sprinkle: Was there conversation with the doctor?

Diane: Either the doctor is not allowed to talk to me or he can't speak English. I don't remember any pain. There is a large complex, like a hospital in size. This is one room, but the inner circle...because this is shaped like a bullseye with rooms folding into other inner rooms. This is the inner part of the ship for safety purposes. My Special One explained that to me.

Dr. Sprinkle: Anything else?

Diane: There are muted silver colors on the walls, and machines almost like a dentist's office. The ceiling is not too high, maybe

23

seven and a half or eight feet. It's large for an office, though.

Dr. Sprinkle: What does the doctor look like?

Diane: I think the doctor is darker than my Special One and taller, maybe five- eleven or six feet. He is very gentle.

Dr. Sprinkle: Equipment?

Diane: Just an x-ray kind of thing. I don't know if it was used on me. I didn't feel anything. There was no formal medical examination that I remember.

Dr. Sprinkle: The doctor's garments?

Diane: He looked "medical," had a cloak or gown type of covering. He is older than my Special One, but has the same glistening intelligence and gentleness, although I could only seem to relate to my special contact. Perhaps channels were just not open to anyone else...I don't know. These people have such a high...awareness...it literally shines in their faces.

Dr. Sprinkle: Tell me about other encounters you may have had.

Diane: There was this large mothership and shuttle experience in San Diego; I have a friend there who is connected to my Special One's alien companion. I was riding in the car with this woman...it was April 6,1979...we had gone out to look for UFOs or for some trace of the souls we are connected to. We got in her auto, drove to Black Mountain, and she kept looking for a strange car she had encountered before. We were becoming impatient (deeper hypnosis) and then we saw a bright light or object, moving, and...oh no...a smaller lighted object is headed right toward the big one. They're going to crash...but no,...they merge! And then the big one flies off so fast, so fast.

Dr. Sprinkle: Was there a time lapse?

Diane: Not that we could figure. But, I found it difficult to talk with my friend about this experience, like, I wasn't supposed to dig into it. I know these ships held our contacts, but maybe they were doing something else in the area at the time. Maybe they

24

were saying: "You came all the way out here, but you needn't have done that (I was living in Florida at the time and visiting San Diego), but what you have is special only unto you. Keep what is yours." I don't understand that message entirely. The event was also the symbolic melding of the "smaller" into the "larger." It symbolized my own developing awareness and connection with my space contact. I felt that they...or the overseer of the experiment was aware of my sudden intense surge in psychic awareness. He was pleased, as if I am a good student. They felt a little surprised that I had managed to trace my roots so accurately and to remember them so well.

Time: 2:50

Dr. Sprinkle: Any other impressions?

Diane: My Special One, I want to return to talking of him. It is like a black screen dividing us. I know the feeling I mean, but I can't get it into words. Like
the other side of the coin...it's an integral part of me, he is my souL.and yet, how can one side of the coin ever touch the other side?

(Comment by Dr. Sprinkle: At this point, a few minutes before 3 o'clock, Diane starts to renew her crying as if something has once again touched her emotionally.)

Time: 3:00

Dr. Sprinkle: Any past life memories that might help you?

Diane: I have visited my life as JohnLocke before. He was not the well known philosopher, John Locke. I was a young Englishman from the country. It was 1791. I had much growing to do. I was a loner and an army deserter. But, I was a gentle one, I did not belong in that time. I was out of place. I didn't play the human games correctly. My father had died and mother loved my younger brother Paul more than she did me. I left home at 14 and worked as a carpenter. I accidentally joined the army when I was drunk one night. I hated it and deserted, hiding out in the English countryside for a year and growing spiritually. But, I was caught and kept in an apple cellar in London (I'm not sure why I wasn't in a regular prison). I was not to die for my "crime," but I was stabbed very unexpectedly by my jailer who came in drunk one morning. He was bringing me my breakfast, but started being abusive, saying I was feminine because I wouldn't fight. He pulled out his saber very quickly, on impulse, and stabbed me in the stomach. All I felt was surprise.

Dr. Sprinkle: How does this relate to your present life?

Diane: I have learned to control emotions more than John did. He, and thus I, have learned how to be alone and yet happy and self sufficient. I learned the stupidity of military and establishment thinking. I learned to do my own thing, but unlike John, to do it legally without crossing the law. I learned how to charm my way out of situations. He didn't know how to charm, he was brutally honest. I admire that, but I learned that it doesn't insure survival. John haunts me because his death was quick and violent, and like a ghost, he was left surprised and never really knew he had died.

* * *

At this point Dr. Sprinkle's hypnotic session came to a close and I returned to my normal level of consciousness.

3

GHOSTS: ENTITY ECHOES

Thus the session ended at 3:00 P.M. and I felt as though I had been Home...home to my spiritual star roots and that I had once again been close to my childhood Special One...as well as to John from my soul's last past. Of course, my soul has lived other lives as well, but John haunts me more than the other past lives I have re-visited through hypnotic regression (each memory of imprints made from past lives has been an illuminating and rewarding experience). John haunts me because he died so quickly and violently; he was literally surprised over his death and caught in a "time warp" of not believing himself dead. Someday I intend to travel to London, England, because I am sure that I could find the cellar where he died (or the area where it once stood). I am sure that I would encounter his ghost there, even though his actual soul has gone on throughout time and now dwells in me. However, if I could find the "echo" of him in his surprise at dying that dusty morning in the cellar which smelled so pungently of apples...then I might liberate that echo of him (and myself) and it/he could fade on into the dimension where he now belongs. It must be terrifying to live in eternal surprise, not internally knowing that you are "dead," yet not able to interact with the world around you.

I believe that all ghosts are "echoes," that their actual souls have all gone on to other lives and realms but that, similar to radio waves that eternally orbit the Earth, the surprise of being "dead" leaves an emotional, soulful echo which can materialize into the body pattern the echo possessed when it "died." This is why ghosts often can be traced to a violent and unexpected death. An echo is created which a more normal, slow, expected death (for instance, from a disease), would not create. In the case of an expected death, the soul can usually hold itself together in its entirety, creating no "footprints" or echoes as it leaves. No consciousness is left in limbo.

These echoes are not the original "voice" of the soul. In other words, if you call out "hello" on a mountainside, it is the echo of your voice which returns to you again and again...and not really your voice. You still have your voice in its entirety. And so, I am not suggesting that my soul - or the soul of anyone else who might have become a ghost in a past life - is not whole in this life. It is whole! It is not fragmented! However, the echo of me (John) at that time and place is caught in an eternal network of "echoes" which create the ghosts we encounter from time to time on this "haunted" Earth with all its ghosts and anomalies.

These echoes are normally harmless though a bit unnerving as they search throughout time for the answer to their "existence." They literally do not know they are dead and continue to go about their lives, passing down stairways on their daily chores or gliding through the kitchen to fix the tea. However, these entity echoes have no souls...but only the memory of one...and so there is no measurable sentience or intelligence. They are merely "motion pictures" of what they once were, natural holograms who look real...and yet cannot offer a soul to prove it, cannot function as a fully charged, conscious entity.

I often think that John's existence and his haunting of that area of London must be sheer hell, but then I realize that he is not me; the essence of John Locke is in me now, along with all my other past life experiences and imprints. It is not really John Locke haunting that London cellar, but only his mind's echo. Still, I would like to liberate it someday. I know that I could communicate with the echo and that it would at last face passing to freedom.

ENTITY ECHOES: CAN THEY HELP US IN THE END TIME?

What do entity echoes have to do with surviving the Change Times and reaching the Transformation? Recognizing past lives and letting them help you...and even reaching back and helping your soul in the time frame in which it used to live...is most important in order to come into full touch and communication with your soul. And when you come into full communication with your soul, you will then realize complete bonding with your higher contacts, be they from Time/Space (like my Special One) or from far distant and higher worlds circling their suns.

Psychically reaching back to your past lives not only helps you at difficult times in these past lives but helps you now realize that you are indeed a creature of the cosmos and of time. You are eternal. You have lived before, you have learned through many trials, tribulations, and joys of the soul. Your roots may even go back to an alien planet. Souls can travel (some are assigned) to research and development on other planets or in other dimensions. Other souls are assigned to time travel (a form of dimension travel) on this Earth. These are the roots of my Special One (and therefore myself), for I know him to be from Earth's future.

My Special One, Tibus, has traveled time as well as space in bodily form. In other words, I know that he did not come to me as an astral projection or image. Actual starships and/or dimension craft are involved, and a very physical experiment was (and is being) performed to help some us in this time survive the horrifying times ahead. He is involved in (as he calls it) Reality Engineering. There is a tragic microsecond approaching on this planet's timeline very soon. It is a moment when the usual policy of non-interference by the Free Federation and Higher Realms will be set aside. It is the moment for which the Free Federation and Higher Realms have been preparing us through UFO encounters and contacts and through spiritual revelations and experiences for years.

You recognize yourself as a mystical being. Your soul cannot be sufficiently explained by science or technology. You recognize yourself as a cosmic essence who lives in many dimensions and who is part of All That Is.

You know that you have lived many past lives and that you must continue to explore them. The more you explore, the more you feel the magnificence of the cosmos. You must continue to explore experiences you have had with UFO beings, experiences which may be blocked from your conscious mind. The more you explore, the closer you will come to achieving a new, higher frequency which will indeed make you "cosmic enough" to survive the Change Point and reach your soul's transformation.

4
CHILDHOOD'S INVISIBLE COMPANIONS

Many of us who will survive the Change Point and reach the transforma tion had invisible playmates or companions when we were children:

You were a"loner," often quieter than your friends or acquaintances. You were the first to feed a stray cat or help a turtle which was stuck on its back. You hated to pull apart daisies in the "he loves me, he loves me not" ritual because you loved and respected nature's works of art, and wanted them to remain alive and whole. You loved to be out in nature and could play by yourself for hours, not needing other children.

When totally alone, you could feel the presence of a spirit or spirits around you. These spirits were kind, perhaps a bit curious, and made your very soul feel warm and free. When your mother asked if you were lonely, you answered, "No," and secretly knew you were not alone at all.

My childhood entities were called The Remembers. This was the name they gave me to identify themselves. There were two spirits who composed The Remembers, but one was much closer to me as a helpmate and a friend. He was essentially my Special One (Tibus), who had earlier come to me in bodily form (as remembered in hypnosis with Dr. R. Leo Sprinkle), but who now visited me in astral form. His presence in astral form has stayed with me for years, looking in on me, guarding me from negative psychic forces which warp many children and adults.

The Remembers were not actually my playmates; they never did play with me as fantasy playmates might delight a lonely child. They were simply "there," implanting wisdom and warmth and "hanging around" as if to see through my eyes. They were curious and yet reserved. I could always tell instantly if their presence was with me on a particular day. It was as if they (and especially Tibus) were living a childhood through my eyes, and my emotions. They were also offering guidance and knowledge which sometimes showed up in strange ways: I somehow knew - by heart - almost all the classical songs by the age of three. My family was not involved in classical music at all; somehow, I had these patterns of musical notes already ingrained in my mind. I also found much of the knowledge necessary for school achievement was already in my mind, and I had merely to apply it, rather than learning it for the first time.

Another form which my invisible companions took were "molecular herds." When I was very young, my mother would put me down for a nap; instead, I would psychically summon groups of grey/black particles. These particles were intelligent and friendly. They would circle the ceiling of my room together, then they would abruptly stop, en masse, and "reverse orbit" going in the other direction! They would follow this strange "reverse orbit" procedure often. These on-going encounters were with pulsing, conscious energy fields; indeed, these were pure energy lifeforms!

These were not particles of dust in the sunlight, because I was very familiar with them also. I have never been able to come up with an earthly explanation for them, and besides, within my soul and my psychic third sense, I know that they were not a part of this world but rather, were a part of my star roots.

There are many moments these days when I wish (as I'm sure you do) that the entities who were so close to me in childhood were as close to me today. "Where are they when I need them?" But, fear not, they are still with us. If the mother holds the child's hand forever, the child will grow weak and dependent. They are with us, even now, and will come back to us in full force when the time is right. Don't be afraid to call on them for strength in these times of stress, worry, and grief. They are still with you and they will help you.

MEDITATION EXERCISE: TOUCH YOUR CHILDHOOD CONTACTS

Lie on your back in a comfortable position, head propped up. Close your eyes. Keep them closed. Take 9 deep, slow breaths. Relax. Forget your body. You are your mind and your mind is you!

Open your third eye in the middle of your forehead, above your brow. Look at the "viewscreen" which your third eye shows you. What is the first impression or picture you see?

Now hold that picture and visualize it in detail, studying the intricacies of the scene. Into that scene, allow your childhood contacts to materialize. Invite them into your mind. They can be pure energy forms, they can be human or humanoid or whatever if right for you. Again, allow them to enter your being, refilling your soul, offering warmth, comfort, and strength.

Allow yourself to drift in time while communing with them. Feel a part of their cosmic Oneness - and feel your cosmic roots being filled with nourishment and life-giving energy.

Open your eyes when you wish (and not until you wish), and feel re-born and resurrected...just as a flower rejuvenates when it metamorphosizes from its wilted, dying state, to a beautiful piece of life after water and nourishment.

Your childhood contacts and other spirit guides, as well as your star guardian, are always accessible to you if you follow the path toward your mind in pure form; in order to contact your own mind in its pure form, you have only to meditate, pray, to set your soul free in whatever way is right for you. You must remember that your contacts are always waiting and willing to help you! You have only to stretch out your mind to touch theirs!

5
A CHANNELED MESSAGE FROM TIBUS

Gentle Beings:

This the first time I have given a message to the people of Earth. Like my brethren Ashtar and Monka, my mission is to guide all Earthers who will listen through psychic messages and UFO related channelings. I am also "one of those aliens" you hear about now and then when someone claims "there are extraterrestrials living here amongst us." This is true, beloved. I return to our beautiful starship from time to time, but I also live here on Earth among you and I have been here for the best part of forty years now.

I must tell you, living here in this place can be terrible at times. I have scars on my soul which will not heal soon. I am so very sad, for this once beautiful planet has now been decimated, pillaged and raped. The animals and the forests have been slaughtered. Spiritual evolution is almost non-existent in many of you citizens. Many of your people remain selfish, seeking only money and the "pleasures" it can bring. It does not bring them love, joy, wonder or happiness, and they have no soul strength to fall back on. They grow more greedy, narrow, and evil. They condemn those who don't look or act exactly as they do. They are "holier than thou," believing they know exactly how the cosmos is (very small, indeed, according to them!), and declaring that there is no God, no Higher Truth. How very sad and how very conceited.

I give this message to you now through Diane, because the time for departure is near. I know how you must feel because there are many moments I feel I can't "stick out" my assignment here. There are moments when I plead to end it, to leave this "hell hole" and to return to my beautiful ship. And yet, your mountains are still powerful and magnificent. Your lakes and oceans still live. And there are a few majestic animals left in your forests. Nature has been my solace during my stay here. Nature is a vital force of the cosmic oneness of all planets. Love it, and protect it, dearly beloved. I can and do return to my ship from time to time, and I wish I could take all of you with me for re energizing and rejuvenation.

Now, here is a brief account of my connection with Diane: Her mother had had an ovarian cyst operation at age thirty-nine and was told by her doctors that she could never conceive again. Ten months later, Diane was born. We are most skilled at genetic engineering, something which Earthers are just now beginning to think about.

The scientists of your planet must not have this skill at this point of your Earthly evolution because your spiritual development has not kept pace with your scientific development; a race of cloned Hitlers, or an army of genetically engineered madmen could possibly be created. At any rate, Diane was genetically engineered, partially using my chromosomes. Just as her looks are "golden" and slightly "alien," so are mine...for I am one of those "gold humans" whom Travis Walton and others have encountered. We are the ones who must live here on Earth because we can "pass" as humans. The "ET" type of alien and many other members of The Free Federation of Planets look non-human (indeed, some are not even humanoid), and so cannot mix with your human society.

Let me clarify two points - Diane is not the only genetically engineered human among you, there are others. In fact, some "star people" are just this.

Diane has a surgical scar between her nose and upper lip, down the line of symmetry. She does not remember obtaining this scar, but knows that it was caused by surgery aboard our ship when she was three years old. We used laser "needles" to reach the brain, going back of the nose.

Our purpose in operating on her was to implant an imprint, or replica, of my soul in her. This is the electrical energy charge that makes me unique. This was necessary so that we would have another helper on Earth. As I have told you, there are others among you who have transplanted essences.

This method is one of many used in contacting humans. We use this particular method only on "star souls" who volunteered for a human lifetime; these are our co-workers who are Federation members in parallel lifetimes.

We also practice the "walk in" technique of entering an adult person who has given up on life and who wants to be free of the body.

Regardless of the method of contact, we realize that life on Earth is difficult for the star person. She knows she is not human, yet in all practical aspects, she is human. She must learn slowly and painfully, who she is, where she came from, and where she is going (what her purpose is on Earth). The star person finds herself to be an energy adapter who naturally attracts cosmic energy, then adapts it to daily life on Earth. I cannot endanger our security by telling you where we live now, how often we must move, or the elaborate security measures we have to protect ourselves. If we were to be discovered and captured, can you imagine the implications? Perhaps our ships could rescue us, but the commotion caused by this situation is not what we are striving for.

My partner, who has been here with me nearly since the beginning, shares this mission on Earth. We are here to observe social trends and changes, but we must also be present here on Earth at a very crucial moment in your history. We are pivotal to the survival of some of your people when the great disasters strike.

Diane is also my "eyes," as many of you are the eyes for space brethren. When you are faced with dilemmas, traumas, cruelties here on Earth, we are often looking in telepathically through your eyes, registering the scene and guiding you. When this lovely blue-green planet undergoes disasters and changes, we will, again, be with you to save you.

Those of you who are reading this book are not those who have made this planet so miserable, explosive, and so cruel. You who are reading this book are the gentle beings, and it is you who shall be saved, to become one with us, to fly our ships, to work toward the transformation on Earth, after the disaster.

A few years ago, Diane reached a certain stage in her evolution: she was seeking her roots. No, not as to whether she is German, English, or Kenyan, but as to whether she is star-related. She knew that she must be, but she is the type, like me, who wants proof. (This is one of the spiritual lessons I must learn, "to have faith," as Ashtar tells me). And so, Diane journeyed to Laramie, Wyoming, and underwent hypnosis with Dr. R. Leo Sprinkle, who is a very special man.

At that time, she remembered my visits to her on the remote Iowa farm when she was a child. She was taken to our ship only three times in over seven years of my visits. Once I took her to the terrarium on our craft and showed her the many specimens of flowers, shrubs, ferns, trees, and animals collected from Earth which comprise the forest/park area of our massive ship. This area is one of my favorites, as it helps retain spiritual balance when one is in deep space. As I have said, nature is all-important to the soul; value it and cherish it!

At this time, Diane also underwent certain medical procedures, which are solidly blocked from her mind with the more pleasant terrarium memory, which could be reached through hypnosis when the time was right; and the time was right when Diane visited Dr. Sprinkle. The surgery itself is deeply blocked in her subconscious. Our sick-bay is highly advanced in Earth terms, yet the trauma of brain surgery is one I wanted this young star person not to remember. Does this sound harsh? It is, unfortunately, true. She is also allowed to remember bits and pieces of my visits to her on her parents' farm. She led a solitary existence there: this was our design. Diane grew up roaming the fields and forests and exploring the river banks of northern Iowa by herself. It was very remote and unpopulated and made my visits unnoticed and safe.

Our missions on Earth are probably more complex than even the most aware of you realize. Our representatives have been present throughout your history and your reality, but there are limits which cannot be passed. We have not intervened in profound ways, because every species must be allowed to evolve in its own unique way. We have sent spiritual leaders among you, offering gentle guidance down the right paths. However, despite our quiet nudges, humankind has now flunked the test and we are now faced with rescuing a relatively small number of the species, those with whom we have previously worked. We must now interfere more than is wise, not only to save a few humans, but also to save the cosmos from massive warping. As Earth unleashes nuclear forces, it will affect not only this world but will alter the Spirit World, ripping apart electrical charges called souls, which exist in the full beauty of their being. It could very well rip holes into other dimensions which even our science could not plug, or deal with. It could potentially destroy us all.

This cataclysm will occur, but we will control as much of it as is possible, predicting where dimensional shift will appear and training souls to withstand the strain thereof. We will have our city ships in hopefully safe areas of Time/ Space as disaster strikes, so that we, and those Earthers we save, will be unharmed. We have calculated long and hard, we have used our precognitive psychic gifts to predict this terrible disaster so as to know how to protect you, and ourselves, from it, beloved. We, too, are anxious, worried, tired...especially those of us assigned to Earth for a long period of time.

When a planet reaches the point where it splits the atom, cosmic forces, like our Free Federation, gather around to see if the planet will:

A)   Use this power carefully and constructively;

B)   Use it to build weapons of ultimate destruction;

C)   Discard this form of energy as entirely too dangerous.

Earth has made her choice, and now we wait, hope, and pray that the damage done will be minimal, to yourselves, to us, and to all spirits of the cosmos.

6
THE END DAYS AND THE CHANGE POINT

Even before the End Days, there will be many challenges, many obstacles in everyday living of which we must beware. We are analyzed by "skeptical scientists" looking down their respective noses at us. It is not "psychologically healthy" to dream dreams, to believe in Other Worlds in a very real way, and to know that the EndTime is fast approaching. Oh, certainly, one is "allowed" to go to church, to sit on the front pew, to offer small amounts of money to the church which can be written off income taxes. However, one is not supposed to truly believe, to have great faith, to search the skies at night feeling pure wonder and awe, and one is not supposed to seek one's guardian angel, one's higher self, one's space connection, or one's spiritual roots. One is not "allowed" to nourish the soul to too great a degree; if we do, we are considered obsessed, fanatical, a religious "nut" and a psychic "weirdo."

How many times have you been tempted to tell the world to "get lost" and to just melt into the comforting arms of total meditation, devotion, and soul searching? However, we must be strong and continue to function in this place...until the End Time. If we "give up" or leave our job, or reach a point where we "can't take it anymore," we are giving those skeptical scientists and front pew church-goers and those worshippers of the "god" money, a victory over us. We *are* strong and we can function, earning money for the needs of our loved ones, spreading the word of spiritual truth we know so well. Or, we can remain quiet because no amount of "word spreading" can stop the End Times ahead. Ultimately, it is up to each individual soul to feel the need for enlightenment or to continue on in darkness with no preparation, no conditioning, no forewarning knowledge of the times ahead.

Whether you confirm your feelings of imminent disaster through psychic revelations, through the Bible and other religious credences, through meditation, or through scanning the skies (or perhaps through all these methods!), you feel the call of something"more." If your next door neighbor, or the guy next to you at work, does not feel this need, does not feel this relationship to Mother Earth and Heavenly Father, then there is little that you can do for him. You can present him with your knowledge, but if he laughs or smiles tolerantly and strolls out to have a beer and watch the latest football game, then you can only be strong against his laughter, and feel remorse for him as he turns his back on his soul's need for nourishment. Perhaps his soul is not yet seasoned enough or evolved enough to make its need for nourishment heard.

It is vital that you keep your urgent desire to find "more," and to enrich your soul in order to survive the End Days. There will be pressures - ever growing pressures - to stop this "mania." There will be financial pressures to work an extra job, or to continue a job you dislike greatly, which displeases your soul. There will not be much time for meditating, for seeking spiritual roots, for preparing for the End Times, and training for the tidal wave. However, worldly problems and pressures are also a form of training and preparation and they are making your soul as strong as it possibly can be.

THE RIPPING APART OF SOULS

Will the great disasters really mean the end to life on Earth as we know it? Will it really be so bad? After all, our Space Brothers and Sisters, and those beings of Higher Realms will be there to help us.

Tragically, the unspeakably terrifying forces unleashed during the great disasters will be so mighty that we will need the strength of our own being as well as the welcome, strong help of our special celestial contacts.

The greatest danger of all lies in the nuclear forces which will be unleashed. There need not be an actual nuclear war, though that evil hovers over us like a hungry vulture at all times. Once the dimensional shift occurs and planetary-wide changes begin, earthquakes and volcanoes will shake the very core of the Earth. The many nuclear power plants, storehouses and arsenals around the world will suffer meltdowns and vast quantities of radiation will be released. The natural disasters will be devastating enough, but the nuclear force unleashed is the same as unleashing The Devil himself!

Yes, the unleashing of nuclear forces is, in a very real way, the devil himself! Nuclear reactions split the basic building blocks of the universe. Nuclear reactions mutate energies and electrical charges. All souls are actually unique electrical/energy charges which dwell in an individual's brain, but which live throughout time, long after the earthly body dies. Atomic meltdowns will spell disruption and chaos to those unique energy charges and souls will become lost. An atomic holocaust will mutate and tear asunder all but the strongest of souls. The ultimate evil will warp weaker spirits, leaving meaningless, radiated bits of energy with no consciousness, no soul.

The terrifying fact is, we do not need to have a nuclear was to unleash this anti-life, anti-Christ force. A few meltdowns in nuclear power plants across the globe will be quite sufficient.

Unidentified Flying Objects (UFOs) began appearing at the dawn of the Nuclear Age. 1947 was the year Kenneth Arnold spotted the nine "flying saucers" over Mr. Ranier; at the same time, the United States and the Soviet Union were heavily into beginning experimentation and testing of nuclear devices. Coincidence? No! Our Space Brothers sadly noted that we had reached the point at which all "civilized," technical planets arrive: The Nuclear Age. If a planet is wise, it deserts nuclear power as entirely too dangerous to all life and concentrates on the many other forms of energy available.

Earth, however, was not so wise nor so lucky. The truth is, nuclear power is not just a "stage" in industrialization, but it is the ultimate anti-life power. Other energies do not have the widespread destructive power, cannot obliterate all life and all souls.

If you actively pursue goodness, soul development, and higher contact in your life, if you do not harm nature, if you strive to function while bearing the terrible knowledge that the Change Time is near, if you find yourself dreaming of and longing for the transformation where your soul's spiritual roots await...where reality will be fresh and beautiful once again...then you *will* survive! You will be one with the powers of nature and the Creator. You may survive physically as well as spiritually and will either join the crew of a starship, seed new planets, or lead what remains of Earth toward a golden New Age. Or, you may be freed of your physical body; you may have achieved sufficiently high spiritual development to no longer need your physical body. The energy force that is your soul will become one with the Creator Spirit.

Whatever your unique niche, if your soul is strong enough, you

40

will survive and flower in the transformation!

ARE THERE OTHER
DIMENSIONS? A MESSAGE FROM TIBUS

There are other dimensions, beloved reader! Your most advanced quantum physics now tells you this, and spiritual messages and space channelings throughout the ages have always told you this as well. Most of all, your soul confirms this with gentle stubbornness. Others may laugh at your "science fiction" ideas or "blind faith," but be assured that you are right! Other dimensions do exist in infinite combinations of infinite diversity. Heaven is a spiritual dimension which all souls strive toward as life after life passes. We all (we Space Intelligences as well) evolve closer and closer to this perfect feeling, this perfect place, this perfect, all-encompassing joining with the Creator Spirit.

When the great disasters hit, not all of us will go to heaven, nor will we necessarily want to, or be chosen to go. Some souls have more lessons to learn, more evolving to do. There is also freedom of choice: some of us desire to experience adventures in the stars, or in dimensions that are not as perfect as heaven. It is these souls whom we Space Brothers have chosen to be the crew of our starships, to become one of us, and to return to Earth after the cataclysm to help re-organize civilization and to help any survivors. Many of you "star people" will retain your earthly bodies.

Others of you have already made the decision that heaven awaits you when the time comes. To you gentle souls, I send my blessing and abiding love. Yours is the Kingdom of Heaven.

May the Healing Light of Love and Goodness surround you, always.

Tibus

PREPARING FOR THE CHANGE POINT

Suppose you were hit by a huge wave while wading in the ocean. Suppose you did not have the slightest inkling of how to swim. What would your chances of survival be?

Suppose you were hit by the same wave, but that you not only knew how to swim, but had practiced for years holding your breath, floating with the strong currents, and improving your endurance. Now what would your chances of survival be? In short, we all know that conditioning, and preparation improve survival chances. In what ways can we prepare ourselves for the Change Point.

The Space Brothers and Sisters are much like lifeguards in this situation. They will be helpful and vital to you whether you are a swimmer or not, but we must be as strong as we can be ourselves, and we must have nourished our soul and conditioned our soul to the highest state possible. We must help ourselves!

In order to prepare ourselves, it is essential that we recognize our beautiful, unique souls, in all their glory and trauma, from past lives. We must seek out - actively - our spiritual roots. Many of us find our roots to be Christian, others have Hebrew, Buddhist, or Hindu roots, some of us go back to ancient Egypt or Atlantis, and others of us who are star people find our roots based in the stars in the Future Time. However, all roots relate back to the Cosmic Force and all are part of the Creator. Some call the Universal Cosmic Force "God," others call it Earth Mother, others call it Cosmic Awareness. All are One.

And how are you personally preparing yourself to survive the Change Point? If you stop to analyze it, you are doing more than you think you are! And, you are being guided more than you think!

Do you have one time of the day for meditation, for New Age thoughts, for spiritual communion with Higher Realms? Are there a few precious seconds out of the day when you are "Home," whether Home for you is flying the stars, or abiding in heaven? Sometimes, right before sleep, you may find an opportunity to nourish the soul in these ways. Other times, it is right before you arise in the morning, or in some cherished, quiet moment when no one else is at home, or on a park bench on your lunch break. But at some time during every day, your thoughts turn skyward and toward the upheaval that is to come; then your thoughts turn inward, toward your soul and its spiritual Home. In this way, you are preparing yourself for the Change Point, and the Transformation afterward. You know your soul well and reach its "heart" with serenity and contentment.

You also may receive subtle messages and suggestions throughout each day from Higher Realms. In a very real way, they are looking in through your eyes at the sad state of Earth, and at modern society's daily hassles and human injustices. Occasionally, you will receive an important directive, such as to move to another state, or change jobs. Be sure that messages like these are coming from a pure and good source, and then, follow them! Be aware that many telepathic messages come into the mind without fanfare or distinction and often we are not even aware that we are being guided!

I cannot stress enough that we will all come under criticism for our space and spiritual experiences and beliefs from "concerned" friends and acquaintances. Don't let them divert you from your appointed path! You are more important to the future than you can possibly imagine! Be strong!

DIMENSION SHIFT

A MESSAGE FROM TIBUS

Normally, dimensions are safely separate, intersecting in many infinite number of points, but in such a way that they are not overlapping and they are not entering each others' realities.

Some of these dimensions are accessible through psychic (astral) travel, but the physical molecules of these often bizarre, sometimes beautiful, occasionally frightening worlds, are comfortably fixed within the confines of each separate dimension.

However, when planet-wide catastrophes occur and when nuclear holocaust has taken place, dimensional atoms become mutated and literally transform themselves into the atomic and subatomic particles of new, alien dimensions.

During these times, the sub-atomic molecules and electrical/energy charges that compose the soul, and the consciousness of individuals, can be torn apart...mutated...and souls can literally be lost into oblivion.

This calamity can and will happen to those in the spirit realm, and even to Space Intelligences, as well as to you humans, if the nuclear catastrophe is a giant global one.

Your leaders do not know what they are playing with! They do not comprehend the enormity of the evil they are proposing, when they threaten rival political powers with nuclear confrontation! May the Healing Light of Love and Goodness surround you, always, Tibus.

Once you realize that your soul is you, that the electrical/energy charge which makes your mind unique, is energy that has been on Earth and in the cosmos since creation, then you can easily understand how very important past lives are in understanding yourself today, and in strengthening the soul for the Change Point. Remember, that past lives are more accurately perceived as parallel aspects of the whole self!

Imprinting is an all-important concept. All that you have been, all that you have experienced, all that you have felt, all the trials and tribulations that have been yours throughout the ages, as well as the joys, wonderment, and the happiness, are imprinted into that electrical charge which is your soul. Each time an experience occurs, it is imprinted into your soul. Oh, certainly, it is also stored in that computer called the brain, as science so dutifully tells us, but the reaction, the feeling, the consequence of that experience., .is imprinted into the soul itself.

Even physical ailments or wounds can leave such an imprint on the soul that they continue to bother the individual in his or her current life. An example of this is my teenage daughter. She has always been exceptionally healthy and large for her age; however, she has always been bothered by leg and joint problems, even though doctors can find no medical abnormalities or troubles. Through past life hypnosis, it was learned that in a past life, she had been placed on the rack during the Spanish Inquisition. The torturous pain and trauma of this atrocity has been imprinted onto her soul and into her mind. It continues to "haunt" her in a very real way in her present life.

Through a past life search with Dr. R. Leo Sprinkle, I learned that I had been a very powerful ruler, a ruler with absolute power, back in the "ancient astronaut" days. In these ancient times, I was indeed one of the ancient astronauts who arrived on Earth to help humankind. We brought with us tremendous scientific knowledge and spiritual enlightenment. However, we human-like astronauts were not perfect, were not God, and so absolute power corrupted us as we arranged our kingdoms here on Earth (which were supposed to be divisions designed to expedite assistance to humankind). I ruled absolutely, with the power of life and death in my hands.

However, I rebelled at this awesome power and reminded my

space brethren that we had originally come to help humankind. I reminded them that we were now ruling without mercy, inflicting our power on humans, even if it were not for their betterment. My brethren and my people (the humans I was trying to liberate) turned against me for daring to suggest that our power should not be absolute, that we should not think of ourselves as Gods.

They were afraid to kill me for I had considerable psychic powers which could be unleashed even after death, so they threw me into a dungeon and I was left to waste away. I had dared to be a "man," to speak out against injustice, and I fell from power.

Therefore, I now understand in this life certain fears and dedications that exist in my soul. I have a great and unfounded fear of the judicial system, and of prison. I have always championed "justice and equality for all," but have avoided positions of leadership even though I have leadership potential. How very important to the understanding of my soul, that I found these past life truths! I have found other lives which have added to my understanding of my soul, but none left the imprinting that my "absolute power" experience did.

UNDERSTAND YOUR SOUL: TRANSCEND PSYCHOLOGY

We must be careful not to narrow ourselves by letting psychology or other sciences convince us that their answers are the only "right" ones. Psychology tells us that we are this way or that way because our mother dressed us in pink or was overly protective, or that we have personality traits which formed when our father drank too much or was emotionally cold. However, what about the experiences from past lives? Did not they also form your personality (in other words, did not they also make imprinting into your soul) ? And, they imprinted long before the experience from this life imprinted!

Perhaps you died of starvation as a child in India. Perhaps you found a near-perfect spiritual harmony as a monk in Tibet. Perhaps you died in a street brawl in old London. Perhaps, in ancient Carthage, your father whipped you daily. Perhaps you were a brave German who hid Jews in the basement as the Nazis banged on your door. Perhaps you were a disciple of Jesus or an ancient prophet. Only you can know what is right for you, only you can know the experiences you have had throughout the Ages and the effects they have had upon your soul.

Science tells us that these experiences count for nothing. It tells us that no imprinting ever took place because there is no soul. Psychology tells us that there is no life out there, no guardian angels, no space intelligences, no past lives, no enduring spirit. It is supposedly "all in your psyche...your ego, you id..." And yet, the greatest scientists like Einstein and Tesla did not prescribe to the rhetoric and dogma of science as a whole, for they believed in mysticism. They knew that there is more "out there" than science has yet found. They knew that one's soul is a very real and enduring entity. They were geniuses, they were truly evolved souls, not mere mouthpieces of the great "god" science.

Psychology fails to recognize the existence of an infinite number of lifeforms simply because these lifeforms cannot be seen by the naked eye at every moment. It narrowly and ignorantly announces that an entire spectrum of lifeforms simply does not exist; it states that angels, space contacts, ghosts, elementals, and even God/The Cosmic Force are non-entities! How very conceited and pitiful!

Atheistic analysis does not explain one's soul, does not explain the holy spark that makes each of us unique, does not explain the very essence of our being. And it is precisely this quality...the soul...that one must know well in preparation for the Change Point and Transformation. Otherwise, the soul will not be able to withstand the terrible ripping shock of natural nuclear forces which will be unleashed, tearing weaker souls apart into nothingness, with no base, no consciousness, no being.

MEDITATION: EXERCISING THE SOUL

You are a person who is very familiar with the pathways of your mind and who has practiced meditation for years, even without "officially" calling it meditation. In other words, to meditate is basic to your soul. Many of us were old and wise, even in childhood, and knew how to sit quietly, letting our minds (and thus our souls) wander and explore freely the endless cosmic worlds.

You are so busy these days, trying to make financial ends meet, and trying to function successfully in this place, that it is tempting to let your prayer/ meditation time (be it morning, evening, or late at night), slip past. You feel you must do just one more chore, work just a bit harder on business, or catch up on backlogged work, so that special, precious time for you and your soul does not come into existence, night after night (I am using night as an example, because it is my favorite time for meditation). However, it is essential that you keep your precious moments - even if short - for your soul and your inner self. It is very easy, unfortunately, to get out of contact with yourself. You do not feel your soul any longer, nor the effects of the ageless imprinting. Nor do you have any inkling as to where your soul is going in the future. The space and spiritual messages you might be receiving, are effectively blocked by the mundane static and cannot find a pathway into your being. They "bounce off" even though they are intended for you and you alone. Eventually, your space and spiritual contacts will seek out other humans, only because you are so closed to communication! Certainly you might still know and believe that there is life "out there" and in contact, but it means nothing unless your mind/soul are fertile, and open to spiritual growth in preparation for the Change Point and subsequent transformation.

This does not mean that you should neglect your business, family, or recreational time! It does mean that one must remain actively involved in soul enrichment...if the soul is to be enriched; it is that simple! One cannot be truly happy - or survive - without this vital soul enrichment!

ENGINEERING A NEW REALITY

Have you felt a very real and urgent need to find your spiritual Home, the source from which your soul springs, in the last several years? Has your life been more complex, more hassled than ever before? Do you feel that your soul is being challenged, hurt, torn asunder at every turn of the road? Have you found solace and peace for occasional moments by seeking the spiritual satisfaction that is right...exactly right...for your individual soul? If so, your soul is experiencing "fire drills" both from natural pressures and from stresses of these days preceding the Change Point and also through planning by Higher Realms to condition and strengthen your soul. The Space Brothers, Guardian Angels, and Higher Beings know the hell that is coming and preparation is essential! However, once survival is achieved, there will be peace and beauty in the newly shifted dimension. It is then, we will become one with the Space Friends and move on to a frequency of higher consciousness. The new dimension will be opened by atomic energies; holes will be punched in the very fabric of Time/Space. The new dimension in itself will be a fresh new reality, born out of the atomic cataclysm. This new reality will not be filled with the old wrongs, injustices, bad vibrations and evils that this place has. Man has destroyed nature and our fellow beings; there have been too many wars, too many political power plays, too much greed.

The transformation following the cataclysm will be like riding a cosmic wave and washing up on a beautiful tropical paradise, because, in a very real way, we can make our own new dimension after the cataclysm. Quantum physics tells us that all is Mind. Religion tells us that our soul is the essence of our being. In this, both science and religion agree. And when the great disaster comes, our souls (minds) will be removed from our bodies...as will all souls on Earth (with the exception of the star children who will be bodily beamed up). In the panic of "death" and the joy of liberation from the body following "death," imagine the great psychic force that will be free! It will be the combined force of all minds/souls now inhabiting Earth, plus the great strength and soul of nature herself!

At that time, you will be able to *pick your spot.* If you wish to be in heaven with Jesus and loved ones, so be it If you wish to be among the crew of a UFO/ starship that sails the starry seas, so be it. The fabric of the Universe will be torn open and Mind will be free, Soul will at last be able to find its long-awaited rightful place in the cosmos. Remember, however, that the pressures on the electrical/energy charge that comprises your soul will be mighty! You will feel like giving up, like losing your consciousness and your soul as the cosmic tidal wave rips at your very being. Just remember the transformation that will soon follow, the beauty of the "tropical paradise" which lies ahead on your path, and be true to thine self as the devil tries his hardest to rip at your soul. Know your spiritual roots, know the place your soul calls Home and you will survive...finding your place in a fresh, new world/reality, among the stars, or in heaven itself.

The Change Point is a time we all fear and dread. However, all is in balance and the transformation will be equally beautiful if the soul can survive the great disaster. And since all realities will open up to us as this dimension is ripped apart, we have, at last, the opportunity to return to our true Home, to the harbor for which our soul longs, and has longed throughout the ages. We can return to our spiritual roots, to the cosmic well from which our soul sprang!

WHY DO WE INTERACT WITH THE PARANORMAL AND OCCULT?

You may have *manifestations* which are hints that your space guardian or other higher beings are very literally watching and monitoring you. Here are a few paranormal phenomena which many star people and spiritual contacts experience:

Many of us get buzzings or pulses in our ears and mind right before a psychic event takes place. Recently I experienced a spiritual contact and revelation in a park near my home; directly before this experience, I got a familiar "knocking" and buzz in my ears.

You may have had precognitive experiences. Have you ever know that a relative has died or been in an accident before you received official word? You should recognize here and now that you, dear reader, are a psychically gifted person. If you were not gifted, you would not be concerned about the Change Point. You would not be reading this book about the transformation!

You may have deja vu experiences often, when you know you have been in exactly this situation, said exactly these words, felt exactly these feelings...before. These are flashes which you have had into your own future. Our beings are not confined to this time and place as our bodies are.

You may experience astral travel almost every night, yet your conscious mind may not be aware of it. And if you do travel astrally, you may travel into your own future, especially as stresses and strains of the Change Point draws near.

Being a psychically gifted person, you may sense what other people are thinking, be it good or bad and you may possess psychic sensitivity and intuition on another person's nature before you know him at all. Often your *first impression* is extremely accurate.

You may have had experiences as a child with psychokinesis where items flew off a table for no reason. This was caused by your, then, untrained psychically gifted mind reacting on material objects around you.

It may surprise you to know that many people have none of these abilities. You take them for granted at times and your gifts can be a factor in your alienation because you see through crystal clear eyes when society expects you to keep a "blind pose," concerned only with shallow materialism.

YOUR SPIRITUAL SOULMATE

Do you feel an urgent need and longing to find your cosmic soulmate? Your "twin flame" is someone with whom you can share everything, someone who knows the beauties and, yes, even the ugly corners of your soul. Your soulmate loves you completely, totally, and eternally, always touching your soul, always there to turn to, always yours in a very special way. Do you long to make a new reality with this person or to return to the beautiful world from which you both sprang?

Of course, the soulmate is always there for us if we turn to Jesus because, for many of us with Christian roots and who find the Christian path to be our true spiritual Home, He provides eternal fulfillment of the soul and spirit.

However, others of us who are also spiritually-oriented and who know the Change Point is near, and who also long for soul nourishment, do not find our roots or our soulmate along Christian paths, although we love and respect it and gain infinitely from it.

An important psychic and spiritual fact is that many of us have several soulmates or even vast numbers of soul companions who, all together, form one very beautiful, vital, eternal soul. Many of those already in the Higher Realms are a part of a mass soul which radiates love and energy. These mass souls can pull apart and enter an individual for a lifetime or two...or more. These souls fragment as a means of growing, of experiencing, of helping humankind, for they are always advanced, loving, gentle souls when placed in individual humans. However, a fragment of a mass soul is complete in itself and always has the choice of returning to the Master Soul (the rest of the mass soul) when it wants, after one of its individual lifetimes is over (and the body it inhabited "dies"). It also will psychically and spiritually feel the pull, the desire, to rejoin the mass soul as it continues along its way by itself. It can never be totally parted from the mass soul and can "hook to it" at will through meditation and spiritual fulfillment.

Others of us have one soulmate whom we have known in a past life (or in many past lifetimes); he or she may well be in our current life in some vital, loving roll. For example, perhaps you have (or had) a grandmother with whom you are very close. The two of you always "hit it off" and can talk of your inner feelings and reactions more intimately than you possibly can talk with anyone else. It is likely that your grandmother was a loved one in one of your past lives as well, but she may have been a beloved mate in that life, or a special childhood friend. If your grandmother is "dead" now, she may well come back to you as your newborn child or re-enter your life as a dear friend you have yet to meet.

A dear friend of mine was recently killed in a tragic automobile accident. This woman had searched a lifetime for her soulmate and was finally drawn to India. She psychically felt that she was being guided to that awesome country and that she would surely find her twin flame there. Indeed, she did! He is a young man in Bombay. They recognized each other instantly and spent many precious hours together. They did not relate on a physical basis because, in this lifetime, he is married. However, the relationship was all that they had both dreamed it would be. Now she has gone on to Higher Realms and I know that she is lonely for him...and he for her. However, in future lifetimes, they shall once again find each other and know the pure joy of togetherness.

Sadly, some us are going through this lifetime without our soulmate. We search, and our longing is great. Sometimes we feel we have identified the soulmate but in fact, we have made a mistake, blinded by our urgency and need. This can lead to great hurt which is imprinted on the soul forever...but the soul grows from all experiences. One must feel one's way along, follow instincts, and not be afraid to take a chance in identifying the soulmate. Make the leap. Probably your psychic and spiritual instincts are correct and great joy and fulfillment will come into the otherwise lonely lives of you and your soulmate, for he or she is seeking you as well! If you are from a mass soul, you may have found members of your Home Soul in this lifetime who are, in a very real way, a part (mirror reflections) of your soul's companions and counterparts.

Some of us are lone entities with no soulmate or Home Soul. Lone entities are of equal worth and are very strong, magnificent souls.

For reasons unknown to us at this time, some of us are totally alone in this time frame but know that there is "Home" with other souls who are our twin flames. Some of us have not found other members of the Total Self in this lifetime. This is very sad, but be patient.

Some of us feel a warm relationship with our beloved pets. It is comforting to know that if your ties with them are strong enough, you may take them (or their pure, loving souls) with you as you survive the Change Point. Their life forces are not as strong as yours and they will panic. With the strength of your mind, command them to cling to you, their loving human, and they will be with you as the transformation occurs. Nature is a vital part of The Creator and animals are loved and cherished by the Creator of All Spirits. It is not "foolish" to hope to take your pet with you to the transformation!

Of one thing we can be sure! When the Change Point comes and the transformation is at hand, and as new dimensions open up under the tremendous strain of natural and nuclear forces, soulmates will be reunited, mass souls will come together in full joining again. That combined strength will help all of us to survive the cataclysm and to be transformed into a beautiful new world!

8

WANTED : ADAM AND EVE FOR FUTURE GARDEN OF

EDEN

Being one of those who is in contact with Higher Beings and who will survive to see the transformation (indeed, dear reader, you *are* the Transformation!), you are also one who loves and respects nature. You realize that there is more to the Life Force than most people perceive or even imagine! You know that humankind is not the "highest" entity in this or any other world.

You also know that nature's creatures have the right to life just as humans do. You know that, much like another global disaster in Noah's day, each species of animals will be saved when the Change Point comes.

Many of the Space Brothers' motherships and magnificent "space cities" have established menageries - very enlightened zoos - where Earth's creatures can live in safety and natural comfort. Of course, this also includes transport ing to these large "forests in space" the indigenous plants, insects, etc., on which the animals feed and which form vital ecological chains just as we have here on Earth (or had before humankind interfered and destroyed many vital links in the ecological chain). Of course, these "forests in space" are maintained under giant climate-controlled domes which are part of even larger space ships and cities from which our Space Brothers carry out preparations for the transformation.

In fact, some of the animals which are already extinct here on Earth still survive in relatively small numbers aboard motherships and space cities, receiving special care and are even now being seeded on planets which are being newly developed. On these planets, the animals will once again have the divine right to life without man's evil to jeopardize their existence. They will have a chance to reproduce and will once again fall under nature's laws of survival of the fittest and natural selection so that their numbers are naturally controlled and balanced.

Some of us survivors will be seeded onto newly established "Gardens of Eden" after the Change Point on Earth and we will have newly assigned missions of protecting, nurturing - and being a part of - nature, just as we attempt to do here, though the battle is a losing one in this time and place. Which of us have been chosen for this vital mission? Who are the Adams and Eves among us? The answer has a practical base: Those chosen for this task are those who have a natural aptitude and inclination for living in nature as part of nature; the future Adams and Eves are those of us who can physically, as well as spiritually, establish camps in the wild, till the soil with pride and hard work, and who can communicate with nature and her creatures. Each of us who will survive has the perfect "niche" and it is for this perfect niche we are being groomed by Space Brethren.

For the future Adams and Eves among us, life will be difficult but also very challenging and rewarding. We will at long last be truly harmonious in nature and at peace within ourselves in a way that we can never obtain while trapped in mundane jobs and worshipping the great "god" money here on Earth as the Change Point approaches. For those of us groomed for this mission, these brave new worlds will be the perfect answer for which we've ached and longed these many years as we gaze at the stars and the distant planets which will one day be Home.

Millions of years ago, another Adam and Eve were seeded onto a brave, beautiful, fresh virgin world which became known as Earth. The cycle is never- ending and inspiring beyond mere words. Our souls can feel the wonder of it all when our tongues and brains fail us in adequate expression.

And for those future Adams and Eves among us, be assured that your brave new planets do not necessarily await the fate that awaits the once-beautiful Earth. Reality can be engineered, fate can be changed through the intelligence and spiritual awareness of the inhabitants of each world.

BEING AWARE OF THE POWERS OF NATURE

You may have a beloved pet or pets in your home; even if you don't have pets, you would not be one to abuse or mistreat them. You realize that animals are - in a very real sense - our brothers on this planet. Their company is comforting and they provide a very pure friendship and love with no questions or restrictions. Recent studies have shown that people confined to homes for the aged respond more positively when allowed to have a pet to pat, to care for, and to love. It gives their seemingly useless lives new meaning. Once again, they can establish contact with Nature just as they experienced in their childhood. They can feel their soul blossoming and responding to the love and need the animal feels for them.

There is an ancient Pagan saying: What goes around, comes around. A more positive way of stating this truth is: Do unto others what you would have them do unto you. While humankind possesses technical intelligence far beyond that of animals, and therefore should have felt it his role to love and protect them, man has instead hunted them, often skinning animals for the beauty of their fur so that a huge financial profit could be made. Man has not hunted animals to feed his family, but rather for the "sport" of it. He has slaughtered them cruelly and mindlessly, butchering these precious lifeforms totally out of existence (in many cases). Man kills babies and adults alike, using his intelligence negatively to "outsmart" Nature's creatures as they hide in their forest-carpeted homes.

Now, the nuclear cloud hangs over man's head. His cities are crime- ridden, over-populated and miserable. His oceans are polluted and his rivers are dying. Still, man continues to cement the meadows, to cut down the remaining forests, to butcher the animals. However, nature does have a way of "getting even!" Nature does possess intelligence which is intricately connected to the Creative Forces (and to The Creator, therefore!) Earthquakes, tidal waves, volcanoes and great fires will soon be unleashed which will have a fury not seen before on the face of this planet. Nature will beat man down, making him see clearly in his dying moments that he was indeed a part of this once-green, once-beautiful orb in space. He should have acted as Preserver and Protector...but was instead, the Destroyer.

Unfortunately, man's discovery of the nuclear force may well reap revenge back on nature, as earthquakes and upheavals loosen atomic stockpiles and meltdowns occur. Will nature, herself, die on this planet? Nuclear power is anti-life, anti-Christ. No life can occur after it has paved its deadly path for millions and millions of years.

The Space Brothers and Sisters have no choice than to save some of us, just as they will save representatives of each of the animal species. They cannot interfere so totally as to stop the destruction. It simply is not possible, even for them. Besides, fate has decreed that humankind will reap what it has sown...but those of us who do not deserve to be punished will not be.

EXERCISING: PHYSICAL PREPARATION

You know inside yourself if there is a pressing need for physical nutrition and exercise in your life, or if you are more inclined toward mental/spiritual/ psychic pursuits. In practical terms, those of us who will be bodily taken into the ships, have a need to be in top physical shape. Physical regimen on board starships is routine and mandatory. We will be trained to operate the ships (US-FOLKS will become UFOLKS, as Dr. Sprinkle says). Also, many of us will be returned to Earth, or seeded onto new planets. These Adams and Eves will have to be in top physical shape. Exercise and diet are most important to all of these groups of survivors.

If the physical aspects of life mean little or nothing to you, you will likely not possess your body as you know it, after the Change Point. Your soul is ready to exist on higher planes which do not require cumbersome physical bodies.

Because I am one of those who will be trained for living and working on starships, exercise and diet have always been most important to me and I am convinced that it is part of the implanted vision and knowledge I was given by my Special One...for the transformation. I am a skilled gymnast, simply because it is in my soul to be. The exercises have brought me spiritual serenity, much as yoga does, as well as keeping me physically fit.

9

EXTRAORDINARY PHENOMENA
UFOs IN THE SKIES

In my adult life, I have had four excellent UFO sightings. I use the term "excellent" because they are all scientifically good sightings. I have investigated each thoroughly, searching for worldly explanations of IFO (Identified Flying Objects) answers. None can be found.

There are about a dozen other sightings which I've experienced which are uncertain scientifically. I personally feel that the majority of these were bona fide UFOs as well, but because of the brevity of the sightings, or because of the IFO possibilities, I will not discuss them in this book. Instead, I will tell you of the four which defy earthly explanations and also relate to you then- special psychic significance and message for me. Each sighting/encounter/ experience, was unique unto itself, in both physical characteristics and significance for me.

In the spring of 1966,1 stepped out on the back porch of my home in St. Petersburg, Florida, to gaze at the stars (star gazing is a necessity for me, just as drinking water is a necessity. I gaze at the stars and know I am gazing at my Home. I know that I have actually sailed those starry seas, and that I will someday, again). As I turned my sight upward, I saw two absolutely beautiful "manifestations" directly over my house. I use the word "manifestations" because this was the least physical of my four sightings. No solid craft could be seen, but a spiritually positive feeling swept over me and I could not take my eyes from the breath-taking sight in the heavens. There were two energy sources in the sky which formed perfectly concentric circles of many unearthly "electric" colors. Each circle within the larger circle was a different color. The two large circular areas were exactly the same in the patterning of their colors; I cannot remember the exact order of the colors, but the colors involved in this beautiful sight were red/purple, gold/orange, and yellow/green. I know that I was looking at pure energy!

The scientific side of my nature thought of a temperature

inversion or some atmospheric condition to explain this lovely sight, but my soul knew that my special childhood space contact (who even now, is channeling through me) was "activating" me in my coming adult life with a promise of circular, all-encompassing, celestial protection, guidance, and energy. This was the re awakening, the second birth of my mission here on Earth. The knowledge and gift-of-soul I had obtained in childhood, had been dormant until this night when, at age nineteen, I was re-activated for my on-going mission before the End Time.

AN EXPERIENCE WITH "THE ONE"

In 1979,1 encountered my most startling and sensational UFOs on a dark night along a mountain road which is steeped in psychic lore. I had journeyed to San Diego, California (where I live now) from my home in Florida to visit a close friend who has experienced many of the same phenomena and feelings in her life as I have. In reading Dr. Sprinkle's notes on my hypnosis, you will find that my Special One has a soulmate and "partner" on his unique mission and that this non-human (his companion) oversees the mission.

My friend had had other bizarre experiences along Black Mountain Road and so we drove up and down the five mile stretch of road hoping to encounter "our roots." We had the CB radio on and just at the far point of the road, before it winds toward the small development of Rancho Penasquitas, we heard a frenzied voice come over the CB, yelling a name three times. There were no other words, just the name. It was the name of my Special One's companion who oversees the mission.

My friend and I were scratching our heads, trying to figure who or what we'd heard. We both knew perfectly well that we had heard a very special name come over the CB (and the person yelling the name seemed to be in desperate trouble), but we tried to reason it away be saying perhaps we had heard Spanish or another language conducting a perfectly normal conversation. However, we knew otherwise.

We continued to drive as we tried to figure if our imaginations had run away from us. We had gone nearly a full round trip, heading back down into the middle of Black Mountain Road, going toward Rancho Penasquitas again. At the most remote spot along the narrow road, I looked to the west, along

the side of the mountain and there, low in the sky, was what looked like an intense, bright planet. Since it was moving, I reasoned that it was a plane, though a strange and wonderful feeling was creeping over me. I continued to watch the light carefully and my friend watched it as well as she could while driving.

Suddenly, a smaller light, about the intensity of a moderately bright star, appeared in the sky heading directly for the larger light. I barely had time to express my fear that the two "planes" would collide, when the smaller light sailed directly into the larger one! There was no hesitation, no slowing down; the smaller light was "swallowed" instantly! And in another split second, the larger light shot off, flying directly over the road in front of us. As it sped over the car, we could see that it was a brilliantly lighted triangle! These were not the tail and wing "triangle" made by planes but an actual flying triangle with super-intense lights. The craft made an abrupt right angle turn and was out of sight instantly!

Obviously, this was not a tanker/jet refueling exercise (I investigated that possibility very thoroughly). While San Diego is prime military air space, we have never before or since seen lights like these. What machines does the military have that behave as these did?

To put our sighting on Black Mountain Road into "space" terms, the shuttle (saucer) approached the mothership, the shuttle bay was opened, the shuttle flew in, and the mothership zoomed off! There is no other logical explanation! And it is my psychic understanding that my Special One, Tibus, whose voice we picked up on the CB moments before, was in the shuttle and was in urgent need of being picked up, for some reason. Telepathically, I feel that the near-by military base had been alerted to his presence in the area and was about to give chase.

The significance of this sighting was slightly less comforting than the concentric energy forms thirteen years earlier. I feel that this sighting signified that my friend and my lives are "tied together" just as my Special One and his companion are "tied together." It showed us that we are on the right track in our intensive discussions, channeling sessions, meditations, and pursuits of our star roots. It also left me with a feeling of worry and aloneness: Worry for my Special One and aloneness within myself. I cannot explain it further but it was an "uncomforting" experience, though essentially a positive one.

THEY DANCED IN THE SKY

In March of 1980, I was driving home from a session of past life hypnotic regression with a friend, Shirley, a medical hypnotist. In the sky about a mile
ahead of me were two dancing, pulsating red lights! They were literally dancing and cavorting in the sky, staying ahead of me, which put them almost over Tampa Bay. Keeping one eye on the road and one on them, it seemed they would not let me gain on them in distance. One would hover for minutes on end while the other swung back and forth, pendulum-like, underneath. Just as I would think I was approaching the area they were over, they would dance onward toward the south. I analyzed their antics and could see they were not helicopters, planes, or balloons.

I headed quickly for the park which overlooks Tampa Bay, near my house, thinking that I should get out of the car and observe these two "silly" lights carefully. Just as I arrived at the park, the lights stopped their somersaults and flew straight across Tampa Bay at a very high rate of speed. They were out sight within seconds.

I was very frustrated but the message I received, telepathically, was an interesting one: I was so-near and yet so-far from completing my mission. I was (and am still) too impatient. They wanted me to know that they were "around" but that I needed to go the distance myself, too.

PULSATING DISCS OVER TAMPA BAY

My most significant sighting of 1980 came the day school was out for the year, on June 12th. (I was teaching elementary school at the time). Tampa Bay, like Black Mountain, has high psychic energies, and so I found it fascinating that this vivid and long lasting sighting occurred directly over Tampa Bay.

I had stepped outside at nightfall to look at my precious stars, tired from the chaos of the final day at school. As I surveyed the skies, I noticed two brilliant balls of blue/white light hovering over Tampa Bay. I ran down to the park (the same park where I observed the pulsating, dancing red UFOs). The lights were quivering and flickering low in the atmosphere as Venus does when it sets, if it is exceptionally brilliant. I quickly ran back home to get my star chart to check for planets or stars low on the horizon to the south (though I already knew there were no such twin planets or stars).

My mother and daughter ran back to the park with me and even my mother, who is a UFO skeptic, was speechless and unable to explain these two astounding objects. Cars and people continued to move through the park and we were not sure if they noticed the lights. My investigative nature told me that I should go and ask them about the pulsating balls but psychically I was told "not to bother."

The light to the right seemed to be blinking and bobbing in a way that I felt was representative of my Special One, so silently I attempted mental telepathy with this particular light. I felt the definite knowledge that we were communicating through the soul, that he (the light or the entity inside the lighted craft) heard my pleas to "beam me and take me Home" (this was way before the movie ET!) Many, many times throughout my life, I have asked to be "beamed up" so as I can "go Home" because, like you, I find this place unbearable much of the time. However, I am always told that I must first complete my mission and that the End Time will be my time to return Home.

Just as I felt a free flow of mental communication with the glowing ball to the right, my mother, daughter and I had to turn our heads to step out of the way of a car. When we looked back, one light had totally vanished; it was the one I had been communicating with! It seems a huge "coincidence" that the particular light I was in contact with disappeared in the split second we turned our heads!

The second glowing ball of light stayed all night, winking and blinking, getting greater and lesser in intensity. It did not float away a balloon would do, and certainly neither a helicopter nor plane could stay in one exact spot for hours and hours! My mother and daughter finally went home and though I was determined to watch the light until it flew away or vanished, I felt myself getting very sleepy. I suspect that I was "ordered" to sleep just as with the concentric circles of energy in 1966. The glowing white ball of light was still there, in the same spot, when I left at 1:00 A.M. and fell into a deep sleep.

Why two objects? The significance of that is that the two

wondrous circles of energy reflected the mirror image soul of my Special One and myself. One from two.

I watched these concentric manifestations for three hours, as did my parents. They did not drift away with the wind; they stayed directly over my house. This eliminated the possibility of a military test, weather balloons or a strange atmospheric condition. They did not weaken in intensity, did not vary. Finally, we all went to bed, having gotten very sleepy. However, I have since wondered if we were "ordered" to go to sleep, thus not seeing the departure of the objects/manifestations. I suspect that on a subconscious level as I slept, I encountered further communication with them.

The significance of this sighting was a very warm one for me personally. The intense energy sources were again letting me know that they love me and are watching me. I do not understand why my Special One disappeared when we established communication. Perhaps the time is not yet right; perhaps it is not the time when he and I should meet face to face. The endurance and strength of the second energy source left me feeling strong and confident and at peace.

BIZARRE PHENOMENA: THE BEEPS

Many of us, from time to time, have had very strange happenings in our lives. Others of us do not have them, or at least, not as many of them. Or, our phenomena might have been confined to our childhood days. Whatever your particular case, you know that you do have a very real connection with someone very special, very good, and very strong, who is "out there."

I shall relate a few of the bizarre phenomena which have followed me throughout my life. Perhaps you have had similar happenings!

I had a mysterious one and a half years of "beeps" in my house! From February, 1980, to May, 1981, my house "beeped" at predictable, timed intervals. Star people often get beeps or buzzes in their ears/head/mind right before psychic phenomena occur; this has happened to me on several, supernatural occasions. However, these particular beeps were not in my head, but came from electrical and battery-operated appliances. Other people heard them and my daughter and I recorded them. Unfortunately, they had the strange ability to disappear from the tape after we re-played them once or twice. We do still have several beeps preserved on tape, however.

63

The beeps began in our house shortly after my daughter, Gianna and I were attempting to communicate, psychically, with the Space Brothers, by sitting quietly, concentrating on sending our message of love and peace. The light bulb "tinked" in an odd way, but we paid little attention. Now that I look back on it, I believe it was the forerunner of the beeps. The next time we attempted communication, a "beep" came over the television, which my daughter had left on low volume in the background. Again, we rationalized it away, figuring it was a ham or police radio signal which our television had "caught."

Then the beeps became regular, daily features of our routine. They still came from the television, but also from the wall, the stereo (whether only the motor was on or the music blaring); we also heard beeps in the clock radio, the neon light, a small desk lamp, the space heater, and even the phone line (dial tone) beeped at me as I was about to dial a call. The beeps never came in two appliances at once and they usually "chose" the appliance that was closest to me, if I were sitting still, reading or writing or they would "choose" the appliance closest to my daughter, if she were sitting still while I worked around the house.

Even more bizarre, they started appearing in Gianna's battery-operated cassette recorder! This means that an energy was pulsing through our house which not only worked through the electrical system, but also manifested itself in the batteries of the recorder! Some of the loudest beeps came from the battery-operated cassette recorder! I even took the recorder out under the stars and picked up the beeps about twenty feet away from the house.

There was a definite intelligence behind the beeps, because after beeping randomly for several months, they began coming in at specifically timed intervals! They would come at five after the hour and at thirty-five after the hour. However, they did not occur at every one of those times. In other words, they might beep at five after four o'clock, but might not beep at five after five o'clock or five after six o'clock. They did not come at the same times day after day. Sometimes there would be only one beep and other times there would be one beep, followed about thirty seconds later by another beep of different duration and pitch.

I should explain here that "the beeps" were actually energy pulses or signals coming through my house. They could be described just as accurately as "hums" or "pulses," but my daughter and I developed the pet name of "the beeps," and so they were named.

We tried to communicate with them by pulling the cord in and out right after they beeped at us; we also tried turning the stereo, lamp, radio (wherever they were occurring at the moment) on and off. We were not able to set us a communication system, but it wasn't really necessary, as we could feel a mental and psychic communication.

I journeyed to the Spiritualist community of Cassadaga, Florida, and stayed overnight to have readings and enjoy the peaceful, spiritual atmosphere of this quaint little psychic village. My daughter reported (and caught on tape) that the beeps went wild, the night I was gone, beeping at fifteen after the hour instead of the regular five after, and thirty-five after the hour.

Now I understand the purpose of the beeps, which I did not understand while they were with me. During that year and a half, I grew more and more vitally interested in finding my spiritual roots, in someday flying a silver starship, and in helping the survivors of the End Time. I am sure now that the beeps were merely to intrigue me, to appeal to my acute curiosity, to lead me toward becoming more involved in New Age activities, and...yes, toward writing this book. The beeps disappeared from my home on the day that I read a report on UFO abductions, which mentioned scars of an unknown source on some abductees.

THE SCAR

Nearly all my life, I have wondered about the source of a facial scar I have. Modern medicine has devised a method of brain surgery by going in through this exact spot, and the theory that the far-more-advanced Space Brothers used this technique for psycho-surgery, back in 1947 (the year I was born and the year the saucers first appeared), is not as far-fetched as it might sound to narrow thinkers. I have investigated every possible "worldly" explanation for this scar, and have found none. I have asked my mother, who is a very loving and devoted parent, and who would remember anything that happened to her child if there was minor, corrective surgery on my face at birth. I also asked the hospital to check their records to see if there had been any extra expense for facial surgery. The answers to both inquiries, to my mother and to the hospital, were NO. I suffered no severe, straight, deep facial gash or cut as a child, which I do not remember and my mother is sure that such an accident never occurred. My scar is a deep, extremely straight one and the scar tissue goes through to the inside of my mouth (the scar is small, but plainly visible, if one looks closely). In no way could such a serious cut have happened to me as a baby; my family would remember! Besides, it is a surgical-looking scar!

The scar is between my nose and my lip, and this is the best supplied area of the body; fresh blood rushes through this area and an injury would bleed profusely. If one were cloning, one might take a sample of the best-supplied mouth area to start the clone. However, a doctor can enter the brain by cutting (with a laser or scalpel) this area and proceeding back of the nose to the brain, thus eliminating the huge barrier that the skull represents. This is the explanation which seems right to me, in my unique case.

PSYCHOSURGERY

The mind boggling theory of psychic surgery fits perfectly with my memories under hypnosis with Dr. Sprinkle of something being given to me by my Special One. It was given to me in a medical procedure, which I cannot remember (the experience is blocked by my conscious mind). I believe that his soul was implanted into me (or duplicated into me electronically). I know that there are others out there who share twin souls with a space contact...a sharing that happened through a very real, medical method!

And so, when I read the scientific report on scars of unknown origin on UFO abductees, it all fell into place! The scar I have always wondered about, between my upper lip and my nose, was now explained! I did not need the beeps any longer as physical evidence that, indeed, something "out there" is in contact with me and has been all my life. My Space Brothers have monitored me and - in fact - been a part of my mind, itself, all along! The last beep I heard came over my stereo as I stretched out, thinking of the marvelous information I had learned that day on abductee scars. At last, I knew the origin of my "unknown" scar! As the final beep pulsed over my stereo, I know that it was saying, "Good bye, you don't need beeps anymore. You have your proof (literally) right in front of your nose! It will always be with you, and we will always be with you, and you have no further need of beeps. From that moment on, the "beeps" phenomenon that had been a daily, sometimes hourly fixture in my house, came no more. For those who might scoff at my psychic surgery knowledge, I defy them to explain the scar in front of my nose in a "reasonable" way.

While many of those in contact with Higher Realms do not have unknown scars, others of us do. The star children who will beam up bodily are the ones who have the majority of scars, due to the surgery in early childhood or blood or tissue samples taken in early childhood abductions. It is not an honor nor a disgrace to have a scar due to your contact with UFO beings or with Higher Realms. We have diverse and unique purposes on our survival path through the turmoil of the Change Point. All of us are equal and all of us are one.

THE SKYWAY BRIDGE DISASTER

On May 9, 1980, at 7:35 A.M., the Skyway Bridge, which stretches over Tampa Bay, near St. Petersburg, Florida, was rammed by a large ship. One entire expanse of the bridge collapsed in such a spectacular way that it seemed more like a disaster movie than a real tragedy.

Thirty-three people died in this disaster, as cars and a Greyhound bus plunged over a hundred feet down into the black waters of Tampa Bay. As mentioned before, Tampa Bay has formidable psychic forces and as these deaths occurred and souls were ripped quickly and violently from the bodies, an energy was unleashed that reached my house and entered it, much as the beeps had, through a battery-operated device.

At exactly 7:35 A.M., my smoke alarm began to buzz off and on. It was not the actual fire warning sound (and nothing was cooking or burning any way), nor was it the "battery low" signal. Besides, the batteries were almost brand new. The off and on buzzing sounded rather like Morse Code, with buzzes of various lengths.

When the smoke alarm began buzzing, I was eating my breakfast, prior to getting ready for the school day. My parents and I could not figure out why the smoke alarm was buzzing in this particular way, as it never had before (nor has it since). However, soon bulletins began coming over the radio that a ship had knocked down one entire expanse of the Skyway Bridge and that many people had died. It was then that my parents and I realized that thirty-three people had plunged to their deaths!

I only wish that I had mastered Morse Code, so that I might have understood the message that came through these newly-liberated souls!

I am also reminded how powerful the psychic forces will be as the Change Point rips billions of souls from their bodies. If the deaths of thirty-three people can cause a wave of energy which affects a smoke alarm miles away, consider the psychic energy unleashed as billions perish! No wonder we must nourish and condition our souls to make them as strong as possible to withstand the Cosmic Wave of the Change Point!

LEVITATING THROUGH THE WALL

The summer of 1980, was a very active one for me psychically. My space contacts were evidencing themselves in many creative ways!

One night soon after I had gone to bed (I was not dreaming), I levitated through the wall! My mind was not even on my space contacts and I was not meditating. I was casually churning over the worldly events of the day which had been very humdrum and typical. I was lying on my stomach, as is my habit, when I abruptly felt my body rise up several feet above the bed! There was a choppy, rippling sensation, much like one feels riding on an air mattress in slightly rough waters at the beach. Usually, I am not frightened when paranormal events occur, or when I spot a UFO or receive a telepathic message; in fact, I long for these phenomena to occur (I admit it! However, I do not manufacture them simply to appease myself...how utterly stupid that would be - and such a waste of time!).

On this unexpected occasion of levitating above my bed, I was uncharacteristically scared, and I am not sure why. Perhaps it was because I had never done this particular thing before. Perhaps it was the element of surprise; it was the moment I least expected it. I also have considered that the entities controlling me were not my usual positive contacts, but rather negative forces from the mundane world of elemental spirits, or from the Free Federation of Planet's foes (they do exist!). However, I believe now that I was scared primarily because I was suddenly not under my own control. My mind is stubborn and strong. I will send myself almost anywhere, but I can't stand to be over-powered and taken! Perhaps I needed a lesson in humility and trust.

My night's adventure was not over! I was just attempting to

logically figure out my predicament without too much panic and terror, when my entire body made an abrupt right angle turn, feet first. With my last shred of calm rationale, I realized that my feet now had to be outside the wall! My single bed sat flush against an outside wall of the house. There was no room for my body to be turned sideways and still be totally within my house!

You may suggest that this was an astral journey, but I have experienced astral travel and it was never like this. I do believe that my entire body was levitated and taken somewhere. However, I cannot remember where; I only remember the beginning and the end of the journey!

The last thought I remember as my journey began was, "Well, obviously my entire body is now outside the wall and we are traveling - quickly and with great purpose - toward "

The first thought I remember as my night's journey came to an end was utter panic which screamed, "I must get back inside the wall to my bed!" This part of the journey seemed more under my control because I found that if I tried my hardest, and if I used every ounce of mental/psychic power I have, that I could override the will of whoever or whatever took me. I could struggle over their command and fight my way back into the house. However, I had great difficulty in getting my eyes open. It was a very strange feeling because it seemed that I had two sets of eyes; I could open one set with great effort, but they would not function, could not see the reality I had come from but only a calm, black, other-dimensional place. Finally, after many moments of attempting to fight panic and asserting my own will with all my strength, my "other" set of eyes opened and I was back in bed. Again, this phenomenon may sound like an out-of-body experience and if it were, it does not make it any less significant and real. However, my psychic intuition tells me that it was not an O.O.B., but rather an abduction on a physical level.

I cannot remember the actual abduction at all, hard as I try, both consciously and under hypnosis. I feel that it was a positive, benign encounter, but it left me slightly baffled and hurt that I was taken so willfully and not told the nature and purpose of it.

What was the significance of this adventure? As I've said, it was to teach me humility, trust, and faith - all qualities I need to develop within my soul.

There was a follow-up abduction several weeks later. I had the same terrified reaction though I tried to be level-headed and trusting. This time I was lying on my back, eyes open, and totally awake (as before). Without warning, my bed began trying to dump me out the wall! I was definitely on a tilt and I held onto the bed for dear life! Again, I remember realizing that I was not totally outside the walL.and then I have no recollection of events until the desperate struggle to return to bed.

There was a bizarre piece of physical evidence regarding these two events; our car was parked right outside the wall and I remember thinking that I must be passing between the wall and the car as I journeyed outside the house. On the mornings following these journeys, the battery of our car was drained! The first time, my father had to get it charged and the second time, we had to get a new battery! In many UFO encounters, electromagnetic effects on cars and battery-energy systems are infamous! I found our car's unexpected battery problems (the battery was reasonably new) to be an amazing bit of physical evidence; the car had been a mute witness to my journeys!

Above all, I know that these were not dreams! I know that I have never had experiences quite like these and they were not merely my imagination.

Like you, I am a level-headed person who tends to calm others in panic situations. I do not hallucinate or daydream beyond conscious bounds. I know fantasy from reality. Like you, I know that my spiritual connections are very real.

10

WE ARE AMONG YOU NOW
STAR PEOPLE

This chapter is an introduction for the "star people" out there. Who are we? Why are we here? When did we come? How long will we stay? How do we relate to you? Might you be one of us?

What is space channeling? Is it a new phenomenon in the history of the human race, or has channeling been done throughout humankind's history? How does channeling work? Might you be able to do it (would you want to) ?

What of The Federation? Who exactly are the Space Brothers and Sisters? Are they the same as star people? Do the two know each other? Do they work together? Are contacts with UFOs a prerequisite to being a star person?

In my work as managing editor of UFO REVIEW and INNER LIGHT publications, in my mission as spiritual leader of the Starlight Mystic Church, and in my counseling/guidance work with my fellow star people (and others), through THE STAR NETWORK HEARTLINE and private channelings/ readings, I have encountered many beautiful people who also want to know the answers to these and other similar, urgent questions. Telepathic contact (channeling), and face to face contact with The Federation occurs more and more with each passing year. The star people movement also grows by leaps and bounds as "time" in this 20th Century period flies by so quickly. It is all leading somewhere! This manuscript will tell you the promise, the goal, the mission...of all concerned in this movement (both those in space and those who live on the planet Earth for now).

I am asked so often to explain the definition of star people; almost invariably it is because the person asking the question has good reason to suspect that he or she may well be a star person who has not yet fit the pieces of his or her personal puzzle together, has not yet remembered consciously...the star mission. Also, though the term space channeling is used frequently, many people wish to understand this term more clearly. Seldom is it truly defined or explained. I (and my space contact, Tibus) will explain this to you, in detail.

There are lists of star people's physical characteristics. How relevant are these? Have more traits been discovered? Are there also mind/soul characteristics unique to star people? Is there a common thread in the behavior patterns of star people from babyhood onward?

The format of this chapter is unique. Tibus, my space contact, and I will both approach each subject in a kind of point / counterpoint. The knowledge you will gain will be from the space brother prospective, and from the star person perspective. In unison, balance, and harmony, we strive to make this more than a "primer" on star people but also a handbook for *all* those concerned about the future of planet Earth, for *all* those fascinated with the future, the stars, the higher planes of existence!

In the first section of this book, I detailed the encounters and events of my life and so will not review them here. Suffice it to say, that my life's path has not been an "average" one. In childhood, I was contacted three times; these UFO encounters were not frightening, but instead, quite the opposite: I felt as though I were truly HOME during these experiences.

During these contacts, I met and communicated with my "Special One," Tibus. Through psychosurgery (a medical field which 20th Century medicine is exploring even today), he and I share consciousness. This phenomenon has also been described as: "sharing brain/mind waves;" "on-going telepathic contact;"

and sharing an "implanted essence." These terms, and our explanations of them, will be explained fully within these pages.

Not all star people have remembered contacts with UFOs, and still they are very much star people. They have always felt out of place and painfully different in the 20th Century, on planet Earth. They do not know how to - nor do they care to - play the "games" which must be played for survival's sake on 20th Century Earth. They cherish all life, holding animal and plant life sacred and finding great joy and comfort in nature. They veer away from organized religion, realizing that it is much too narrow for the universal wisdom and law and for the cosmic God-force which is "out there" (and which also exists on Earth)! Star people do have special ones, just a Tibus is my Special One; not all special contacts are UFO occupants. Some are "guardian angel" energy beings. One thing is sure: all special ones are co-workers who supervise and guide the star person through his or her Earth lifetime. Star people deplore cruelty and violence in any form, finding the "low vibrations" on 20th Century Earth almost unbearable. They foresee nuclear catastrophe, and the pollution / contamination of this beautiful planet if there is not a spiritual awakening and upgrading to a completely new and higher dimension/frequency (these terms will be explained!).

DIANE: STAR BEGINNINGS

In looking back on my own childhood and in learning about the childhoods of other star people, I have found that a star identity and a star destiny cannot be escaped - nor do we want to! We have been on a different "wave-length" from the rest of our families and from the world, since the beginning of this human lifetime!

The supraconscious knowledge that there is a mission to be performed, a destiny to be fulfilled...is with us from the beginning.

We are wise and helpful, even as small children; there is an "ancientness" about us. At the same time, we retain an innocent and childlike quality as adults. We value more a hike in nature than a sophisticated trip to Las Vegas. We value more a kitten with soft fur, than a "priceless" mink coat; as a matter of fact, the hunting and killing of nature's lifeforms is abhorrent to us and is one of the few things which will cause our tempers to explode!

We enter "slide zones" and dimensional overlaps easily without being traumatized or enveloped by fear. For this reason, we have had many encounters with the Space Brothers (our co-workers of the Home Dimen sion) - particularly with our own special one (space contact or guardian angel). We also have experienced psychic phenomena at various times in our lives, be it precognition, clairvoyance, sightings of ghosts, telepathy, telekinesis, sightings of UFOs or experienced the beeps and electromagnetic effects brought on by UFO activities near us.

However, some of us have been spared the truly spectacular paranormal experiences, living lives which instead interact with other dimensions in the dream / sleep state, lives which are full of symbolism and enlightened thinking, living lives which have a driving need to find out more universal knowledge, lives which pursue the star purpose and mission. Many star people experience both spectacular paranormal events and live lives which are subtly guided and inspired. We recognize and accept all types of star paths as equally valid and of worth.

Ultimately, realizing that you are a star person dawns - form compelling inner feelings, a lifelong search, a feeling of universal essence which will not let you go, no matter how hard you try to be "normal" or mundane. While UFOs or parapsychological experiences may be catalysts, the star person's inner difference is the "bottom line."

As I have told so many star people, it is not what has always been *wrong* with you (though the world around you informs you of this!) but rather what has always been *right* with you!

MESSAGE FROM TIBUS

This is Tibus. I come to you in Love and Light.

In the late 20th Century, in which you now find yourself, research is beginning into mind waves/ particles, unified fields, co-existing other dimen sions, and into the very state of Life itself (called consciousness / being); also, at this very moment in your history, humankind has the technology to develop starships which fly Space/Time. Most humans do not realize that these fields of research are as far along as they are (though they are still in the "caveman" state in comparison to other civilizations). The Earth governments prefer to deal in secrecy and hypocrisy, keeping knowledge and inspiration from the people.

20th Century Earth researchers are finding that different realms (these may also be called dimensions, planes, or worlds) exist on different frequencies, just as your radio stations can be reached on different frequencies of the dial. Mind waves/ particles are analogous to radio waves is this example.

To continue our analogy, let's say that everyone in the neighborhood receives a certain radio station at a particular place on the dial. However, one person in the neighborhood receives a different station when his or her dial is seemingly at the same place. This might be because of a variety of alternatives. Perhaps this person picks up "ham" radio signals; perhaps this person's radio is very complex and is set up so as to receive distant signals instead of the closest ones, or perhaps this person's dial is slightly "off" and so when it seems to be set on the regular station, it indeed picks up a station near the regular one, but not on the same frequency.

Our star people exist on a different frequency of mind wave, a different vibratory rate, they interact with a different dimension. How do they do this? Both because their "radio sets" (their minds/souls) are basically a different "make" than the typical radio and also because, in most cases, there have been "adjustments" made during experiences and encounters (perhaps not remembered consciously) with us of the Home Side (UFO occupants, guardian angels, beings further up the mountainside than 20th Century Earth). Does receiving a different station cause our star people not to fit into the neighborhood as well? Yes, sadly, this is true. Our star people do not "fit in" - ever - in their lives. However, the neighborhood frequency is one which involves egotism, violence, materialism, pettiness. And so, it is good not to receive that "station," no matter how difficult the star frequency / path may be!

And so, when Diane explains that star people feel out of place and that the star identity and destiny cannot be dismissed, she is essentially saying that the star person's mind/soul simply *are* of a different frequency. The mundane dimension is not their souls' home!

I would like to address the mission and destiny subject in a later chapter.

Being an "essence" (may also be referred to as "soul" or "consciousness") from a different frequency, our star people do experience many "slide zones," as Diane puts it. The mind/soul longs to return home; it does not find the unknown as frightening as the violent mundane reality in which the Star Person lives - and so many parapsychological occurrences happen.

Also, we monitor our star people carefully; many experiences either in the dreamstate, or in the waking state, occur because it is time for them to do so.

I am Diane's co-worker on the home frequency. At certain times in her human life, I have interacted with her, so as to nudge her along her star path, so as to re-vitalize her star energy, so as to remind her of her star mission/ destiny. This is my responsibility.

She may or may not remember a particular encounter in her conscious memory. Often encounters are remembered, such as several of hers were, during hypnosis (see transcript of Dr. Leo Sprinkle's hypnotic regression session with Diane). Whether the experience is remembered consciously, remembered through hypnosis afterward, or not consciously remembered at all, the mind/soul *remembers',* the joy, the wonder, the feeling of being *home again* is remembered in the being, in the heart!

This is all we require. The other puzzle pieces will fit together as time passes. This we promise you!

When a group such as our Federation (the Space Brothers as we are commonly known) find the technical and spiritual "secrets" to mind waves, essence frequencies, other dimensions, it is possible to spend lifetimes in these parallel realities (dimensions) and then to return to the home dimension - all remaining as it was when the essence (soul, consciousness) first began his or her journey.

In this way, it is possible to gently nudge a primitive race such as humankind, 1988, toward a more peaceful, elevated reality. These essences (star people) who are "out of place" are very brave volunteers for human lifetimes. Our star people/?as.y *as humans-,* they are on Earth but not of Earth. Anytime any mind/soul elevates itself past the lower frequency, it is indeed a star soul, an enlightened one.

DIANE: WHO ARE THE 'SPACE BROTHERS'?

Even the hardest skeptic would have to admit that humankind's history has been greatly influenced by the mystical, the spiritual, the unseen. This influence has been intended as a positive one, but it is sadly true that the human race has taken many beautiful spiritual philosophies and turned them into self-serving, hypocritical, and even evil doctrines. We will not be concerned with these *warped* positive energies here, but rather will concentrate on the *purely* positive.

Many people accept that Biblical times were special times; these were times when the Son of God walked the Earth, showing humankind The Way. These were times when various people "channeled" The Word of God, when many people became inspired to find Christ Consciousness within themselves as they related to Him.

The Space Brothers have told us that these also are special times. Virtually all prophecies of all religions (and individual prophets such as Nostradamus) have told us that the latter half of the 20th Century is to be the test for the human race.

Is it so unusual, then, that certain individuals receive channeled messages from the heavenly realm, just as people in Biblical times did?

It is downright logical (as well as spiritually inspiring) that Jesus (also named Sananda in Space Brother channelings) and His heavenly hosts still reach humankind today (of all times!).

The concept of angels having wings seems to have grown from humankind's attempt to explain angels' instantaneous appearance and disappearance in various encounters. Always, angels have been described as human-like; they manifest as beautiful humans, flawless humans. Now, it may well be that there are higher beings who have wings...but the point is, humankind has had experiences with "supernatural human-like beings who come and go in the wink of an eye" since human history began. These higher beings' presence is accepted by many people only in the context of ancient times. *The Space Brothers are these same heavenly beings appearing in modem times!*

In ancient times, the human race was less scientifically oriented. They merely accepted that these beings were "heavenly angels." Now humankind refers to space as the "the final frontier" and believes that one day, he will be able to go "out there" (and this also is the Space Brothers' fervent hope for the human race). Now, these angels are called space beings or Space Brothers. It may well be that this description is only slightly more accurate or specific than the ancient definition

MESSAGE FROM TIBUS
This is Tibus. I come to you in Love and Light.

I wish to channel some additional information on the subject

77

Diane is covering.

To put it succinctly, our star peoples' mind/souls (remember the radio set analogy) are capable of contact with us, the same heavenly hosts who worked with the human race in Biblical times, in ancient times even before the days of our blessed Sananda, and in times since. We have never left you!

We never tell you that our star people are a "closed group" or a "chosen group." Anyone can have the key to the kingdom of heaven. Yes, our star people are souls whose home frequency is our frequency, but as I have said before, any soul which elevates itself, which seeks enlightenment...becomes a star soul!

Our star people are chosen in that they are answering a call to serve and to seek a higher, more spiritual nature (instead of catering to mundane, cruel, narrow behaviors).

And so, if you, dear reader, feel a surge of inspiration at this point, do not tell yourself, "Oh, that's nice, but I certainly am not a "chosen one" or a "star soul." You have merely to open the door to find the higher realms! (Remember Jesus/Sananda's words, "I stand at the door and knock.")

Because humankind is involved in elementary space exploration at this point, we are referred to as the Space Brothers. This is very accurate for some of us, but not as accurate for others. However, we like and accept this term.

Because man was of a more fanciful, innocent nature in ancient times, he called us angels. By angels, we know that he meant "pure energy beings of God and of goodness." We accept this as accurate; in fact, ancient man's term for us did include *all* within the Federation, whereas "space going" refers to some of us.

In order to comprehend what I am about to channel, you must remember that the universe is made up of an infinite number of intersecting dimensions; even man's quantum physics states this fact. And so, not only is *space* infinitely vast (that which you view at night) if one goes straight out into it, it is also infinitely vast if one explores even the myriad of intersecting dimensions around planet Earth alone!

Outer space is much more vast and much broader in definition that science fiction stories indicate.

Keeping this in mind, I will tell you that some of our Space Brothers (I will call them Federation members from here on in) are from the myriad of intersecting dimensions around planet Earth. In times past, these have been called the spirit world. The Spiritualist

Church has channeled these beings for many years; they have guided people individually, giving messages of im pending danger, messages of hope and love. These spirit world Federation members usually work with personal human matters for they have recently spent a human lifetime and can relate to human problems. Many paranormal occurrences which star people experience are caused by communication with this spirit world Federation contact. An example of this is the on-going communication that one of our beloved channels (star people) feels with his wife who passed from the human plane of existence and now works with us Space Brothers (she is one of us).

The question usually arises, "Well, then, is the idea wrong that The Federation are aliens from other planets? Are they really the traditional spirit world which has been reached in seances and in psychic ways for many years?"

The answer is, "We are the spirit world, we are aliens from other planets...and more!" Do not ever make the mistake of limiting us to one exact source! We are many beings of great diversity! However, *all of us are beings of God and goodness who are concerned about planet Earth at this time!*

Yes, some of us are beings from other planets which circle other stars; some of us even look like E.T. of Hollywood fame! As you know, Steven Spielberg based his little alien character on actual sightings of the "alien" bodies which have been retrieved from UFOs (our craft) which have malfunctioned and crashed.

Other extraterrestrial (outer space) Federation members are not nearly as humanoid as E.T. types; of all the science fiction which has been written about variations on life (gray masses of protoplasm, tiny multicellular, sentient lifeforms, rocks which have consciousness, lifeforms which are pure energy/light, etc.), please believe me that it is *all* "out there," and then some! The encounters which await humankind when he enters The Federation are not only more diverse than he imagines but more diverse than he *can* imagine!

However, as man explores outer space, he also explores inner space.

Many of the angels of whom we spoke earlier are spirit guides (Ascended Masters), who are not technically of extraterrestrial origin, not technically of the spirit world (those who have recently passed from the Earth plane). These are beings of the Higher Realms - energies - who call no one planet home but rather serve

79

God directly. These beings are also Federation members, having worked with humankind since time immemorial (the Eastern religions and philosophies have known them well, as have Christianity and other inspired religions).

These angelic beings/Ascended Masters send much of the channeling received by our star people. They are dimension travelers of sorts but their mind/souls are so powerful and so good that no technology is necessary, as God reaches all dimensions, all planets, all worlds.

Another group which belongs to The Federation is, in science fiction terms, time travelers. These are humans of the future conscious level who, through the help of technology (space and dimension craft), journey back in time to guide their human brothers and sisters - before it is too late.

This group is, in one way, the most important Federation group who now works with humankind, for the Future Human Consciousness is exactly what modern man must aim for.

Time may be traversed; it is not a one-way street. Time may be "hopped," various points in time may be visited, for time is made up of multi-consecutive points, all intersecting with multi-dimensions at which we can "Space/Time interphase" (intersect) points (warps).

There are alternate realities to all timelines. Those Federation members of the Future Human Consciousness are those who belong to a timeline where Earth survived the late 20th Century and flourished, spreading her seeds out into the galaxy and to other dimensions. Earth, in this timeline, has become a valued Federation member; we have found that - through mind waves and technical devices which help translate "alien" mind waves - we can communicate freely and with love to the spirit world, the angelic beings, the extraterrestrials, and a host of other intelligent lifeforms including Earth's special natural energies frequently called Mother Earth, and the beloved animal intelligences on planet Earth. In 1988, humanity is just beginning to realize that the whale, for instance, is a wise and sentient lifeform which communicates in intricate ways.

As our beloved Jesus/Sananda said, "I stand at the door and knock." The Federation now knocks at humanity's door. The time has come for humankind to grow up. He is not the only fish in the sea! Spiritually, also, man is not alone!

MESSAGE FROM TIBUS

This is Tibus. I come to you in Love and Light.

First, you must realize that one may transcend the river called "time." Most people on 20th Century Earth accept that time ticks along just as the river keeps flowing downstream and that this is an absolute which can never be overcome. However, with advanced technology and/or with a mind/soul of a higher frequency, one may head upstream just as if you had a motor boat to help you go against the current. Or, one may simply stand on the bank of the river and observe what was and what will be, as well as what is. Also, you must realize that there are other rivers (other timeframes, other dimensions/ frequencies) flowing consecutively with the 20th Century Earth "river".

We of the Federation have stood on the bank of Earth's timeline/history since human life began on Earth. Just as the U.S. citizen should not have gone into the Aboriginal tribe's culture and totally changed it, so we have not overtly interfered with the karmic path of planet earth. However, we do urgently offer warnings of impending danger, we do offer wisdom and insight on the beauty which can be, and we do send in "pre-made" interpreters!

In other words, there are souls among us whose unique essence very much belongs to our frequency/dimension - who volunteer to live on Earth for a lifetime, awaiting contact from us (for this promise from Home never leaves their hearts and souls). This is the only way which we can find interpreters (or bridges) between our dimension and the Earth (mundane) dimension. Unlike the Aboriginal interpreter, Earth simply does not offer a way for tribal residents to get away (leave Earth) for training/experiences elsewhere. Can you imagine a person who had been taken into space by aliens being accepted back on Earth and allowed to advise/help the Earth "tribe" in its problems? The governments of Earth would not even let the "interpreter" out of confinement after his or her experience in outer space!

In a sense, we *infiltrate-,* our star people are on lifetime "espionage" missions. However, these missions are ones which are only to enlighten Earth, to gently guide her, to quietly raise the frequency level, to pave the way for a higher dimension but within

Earth's historical timeline. We do not overtly interfere or change history or meddle unless individual crises do not allow otherwise; and even then we often choose to allow the mundane dimension's karmic debts to be enacted, lived out, fulfilled - so that the higher dimension may occur naturally.

And so, occasionally a star soul is born into a family whose other member's essences belong exclusively to the mundane dimension's frequency. (Once in a while, the star soul is born into a family who has another star person within it.)

This baby, whose unique essence is not at home in the dimension in which it finds itself (a stranger in a strange land!) frequently experiences serious health problems in its early years for the dimension is literally poisonous to him or her.

This baby often has an odd blood type, low blood pressure, low body temperature. However, this is not always the case. An essence from outside the mundane reality simply has trouble adjusting its unique energies to a human body. We do *not* stress these physical differences nor do we stress the unexplained scars which many of our star people have (the result of medical procedures by us during encounters with us, for specific purposes...usually to protect the star person.) We do not stress these characteristics of star people for the simple reason that these are physical differences which could be recognized - and acted upon - in a Nazi-like way by a frightened Earth government, military group, or smaller subversive group. We do *not* want a finger pointed at our star people; their entire mission is one of "low profile" until the return Home can be embarked upon.

The star child reaches early childhood as a human but finds that she (or he) looks at the stars with tears in the eyes - tears which are not fully understood at the time but tears which come from the very heart and soul of the child. These are the stars of Home.

The star child finds that other youngsters function on a more brutal, non sensitive level than she does. She wonders what is "wrong" with her. She turns to Nature for its precious animals, forests, streams, oceans, mountains for comfort and companionship. The star child feels very much alone, very much a stranger in a strange land.

The star child interacts (usually this is not consciously remembered for the child's own good) with unseen companions/playmates; she has dream experiences with the home dimension. Usually, there are also physical encounters with "paranormal beings" and/or UFO occupants. As mentioned before, these are necessary visits by us to our young brother or sister. They are necessary to activate, to awaken the child. The memory of these visits is usually blocked by us from the child's conscious mind (again, so as the child will not stand out as "too strange.")

The star child has a great sense of justice, often becoming involved in human rights and environmentalist causes; however, eventually the star person becomes convinced that a spiritual/vibratory change is the only thing which will move planet Earth forward, for the established governments are too corrupt and complex to change effectively or to change in time to stop global destruction and contamination.

Perhaps the most confusing thing about the star people concept is that no one seems to know how narrow or how broad to make the definition.

Is a star person *only* one who channels a space intelligence, just as Diane is channeling me at the present moment of this writing?

Isa star person *only* one who is extremely wise in metaphysics or UFO data or one whose life is so perfect as to allow an almost total spiritual involvement?

Is a star person *only* one who has an odd blood type, low blood pressure, sinusitis, low body temperature, an extra vertebrae, who was an unexpected child? (I must explain here that often our star people's conceptions occur under impossible conditions, such as their mother being unable to conceive or their father being sterile.)

Is a star person *only* one who has always felt they do not belong to their family? Or, must a star person want desperately to fly in a starship?

The answer to all these questions is "No! " There is no *one* "requirement," no *one* list of characteristics.

It is true that a star person will probably relate to one or more of the paragraphs above.

It also must be remembered that star people's sources (though all of the Federation, a coalition of beings of goodness and God who share a great concern for planet Earth at this time) are not all the same! Some star people do remember, within their very soul...being a crew member aboard a "nuts and bolts" spacecraft (starship.) The longing to return to this home craft is much like a swallow's instinct to return to Capistrano. However, other star people come directly from the "pure energy beings" (angelic

83

presences/ Ascended Masters) who do not use starships.

This example is true for the other characteristics mentioned above. If you do not possess most of these characteristics but *if you have a deep longing in your soul for "elsewhere" and for a bright new day for planet Earth,* then do *not* dismiss yourself as most likely not a star person. You do not need any exact "qualifications;" what you feel *within* is the true test, the true definition. It is very difficult to draw lines between *star people* and *star helpers.* In the final analysis, the soul of goodness who seeks, who wishes to make a better world...is our brother, our sister. Yes, some star people are distinctly "alien," others are not so distinct. It is the spirit which counts!

DIANE: THE SPECIAL ONE CONNECTION

In metaphysics, spirit guides have long accompanied the voyager on his or her journey through the inner reaches of the mind and the outer reaches of the universe.

In spiritualism's communication with the spirit world, other worldly presences have long given advice and comfort (often a trance medium can channel for a loved one who has passed into the spirit world, giving a special message to the relative or friend left behind in the mundane dimension.)

Many people know that they have a guardian angel who guides and protects them throughout their life's path.

Those who are drawn to seek contact with "outer space intelligences" or extraterrestrials often *channel* the wisdom and advice of those higher beings.

Do these descriptions also fit the *Special One* who abides with each star person in a shared consciousness, shared mind waves situation.

Yes, the *Special One* may be thought of as a spirit guide, a good presence from the spirit world, a guardian angel, and/or a "voice" from outer space, or more accurately, from The Federation/The Space Brothers. However, the *Special One* may also be described as the co-worker of the star person, the soulmate, the companion who stays on the Home Frequency and whose responsibility it is to contact, to monitor, to guide, to *stay with* the star person in his human adventures.

In many cases, the *Special One* is simply a crew member

aboard one of the home starships. In other cases, the *Special One* is very much of the angelic realm, truly fitting the guardian angel definition. Again, the *Special One's* exact source depends on the star person's exact source. The Federation's members are varied; the diversity is beautiful, but all beings of the Federation are of God and goodness. All members of the Federation believe in universal law, wisdom, goodness, integrity and in serving the creative God-force.

The star people I work with all know within their hearts that they do indeed have a co-worker, a *Special One.* Not all have found the clearest channels to him or her yet, but spectacular leaps have been made toward this - our most important mission at present if the larger, overall mission is to be fulfilled.

MESSAGE FROM TIBUS

This is Tibus. I come to you in Love and Light.

Again, please remember that all unique essences (minds/souls) function on a certain pattern of energy. The *type* of energy on which they function is determined by the frequency (dimension/vibration) to which they belong.

In other words, "A.C." electrical current might be the type of energy for one dimension, whereas "D.C." electrical current might be the energy for another dimension. This is an over-simplified analogy but it gives you a concept of that of which I speak.

Each mind/soul is unique; however, through spiritual advancement and through technical advancement, we have found that a mind/soul can exist independently in two or more dimensions at the same time. Thus we remind our star people that in a *parallel* (not "past") lifetime, they are one among us, our brothers and sisters, our esteemed and loved colleagues.

We have also found that, through the advancement of the psychic powers of the mind and through technical/medical implants, a mind/soul can be in communication with a co-worker from the home source at various intervals throughout his or her life. This communication can be constant (and we call this a *shared consciousness* with the co-worker/Special One) or it can occur only when necessary (we also called this *telepathic contact*

/channeling).

You must also realize that this shared consciousness and/or channeling allows you to be empathetic with the co-worker/Special One from the home dimension. And so, this is not a mere sharing of cosmic wisdom or facts on possible global destruction, it is an emotional contact as well.

The young star child feels this emotional contact first. The *Special One* who often times has met with the young star child during (what is called on Earth) a UFO encounter - is as a parent to the child. More than parent, the *Special One* represents the link to *Home.* The star child lives on two sides of the mountain: one is his or her life on Earth and the other side is the home side of the consciousness (which is not usually remembered in conscious detail but is remembered always in the heart and soul). The emotional link is the most important connection which the star person has with the *Special One.* This link is felt even if crystal clear communication/channeling is not achieved. This link is all that is truly necessary, though the more finely tuned communication is of course preferable.

The childhood contact may also be termed a spiritual vision or experience. UFOs need not be involved!

There are pre-planned stages which each star person goes through. These stages are known and approved by the star person in his or her parallel life in the home dimension before embarking on the human lifetime. Other facets of the human mission are also known and agreed upon. We stress that our star people are much admired and respected for accepting these missions; there is no punishment involved in living a lifetime on Earth but rather it is looked upon as a noble mission to help save a faltering planet.

In early childhood, the star nature of the star person is very evident. Many interactions with the home dimension occur at this time. The star child usually has three major encounters/experiences with co-workers from home. These may involve UFO experiences or spiritual/paranormal experiences. Usually these experiences are almost totally blocked (by us) from the star person's conscious mind for their own protection; the star nature is sufficient - that which beats in the star person's heart and soul - without their reciting, childlike, an experience which they have had but which no one else believes. This only alienates the star child, hurts the star child...and does not help with the lifetime mission.

The star person does not have an easy time of it in ordinary schools; other children are usually mean to the starchild much as chickens mistreat a quail which wanders into the henhouse. Small beings of any dimension are more "psychic" than adults and sense the different frequency which operates within the star child's mind/soul.

Being more gentle, kind, sensitive, and tolerant than those around you is difficult and results in many hurts and emotional scars. The Special *One* often appears to the star child as either a "presence" which can be felt (a very loving presence) or the *Special One* fortifies the star child's mind/soul, allowing the star child to know that there is truly nothing wrong with him or her...that there is great beauty and intelligence within.

The Special One opens the star child's mind/soul to a very pure communication with nature and with God. Usually organized religion is found to be dreadfully lacking in depth and universalism by the star person, who studies, meditates, experiences on his or her own terms. The star person is basically a mystical being from babyhood onward.

Usually in young adulthood, the star person makes an attempt at normalcy within the mundane dimension. This simply does not work out because it is like trying to get a radio station while tuned to another station; one cannot change the basic frequency of the essence!

There is a time of re-awakening, a time when pieces of the puzzle fit together..after the young adulthood phase is over.

At this time, the Special One re-contacts the star person in a "re awakening." Sometimes the star person undergoes hypnosis, seeking out a reputable medical hypnotist, in an attempt to solve the puzzle of his or her life. Suddenly, the star person *knows* there is a star identity, that there are hidden encounters and experiences, that there is a star mission to be performed. A flame grows, telling the star person that the truth must be found, that mystical secrets must be unfolded, that the home dimension calls.

Often at this time, the star person changes professions or living locations, making an abrupt change in his or her life. This move is very definitely guided and protected by the Special One; a new profession is found which better suits the star nature and the star mission.

At this time, the Special One is sought out in meditation, in channeling, even in seeking out UFO contacts.

Once the full star nature is freed, there is very little which the star person cannot do within the Earth dimension; also, a major step is made back toward the "stars of home." The star nature must be recognized, valued, loved by each star person! Scars from the mundane dimension must be healed, walled off - not allowed to offer a barrier to the star mission.

As the life of the star person unfolds (almost always not along conventional lines!), the star mission is being fulfilled and the Special One smiles.

However, our star people (though many have lived on Earth in all time frames) are on Earth in great numbers during this time frame due to the impending disaster of nuclear confrontation and destruction. Also, Mother Earth (a personification of the Divine Cosmic God within this planet's atmosphere) has been polluted, murdered, maimed by man's careless, cruel hand. And so, the star mission has three phases: one before the Change Point (called the End Days by some), one during the Change Point, and one following the Change Point. I will elaborate on the Change Point in a moment, but I wish to stress now that the Special One is with the star person at all phases of the star mission! 1) The Special One is a loving companion and equal co-worker in the star persons parallel life in the home dimension. 2) The Special One is *the* contact in the star person's childhood experiences. 3) The Special One is the on-going protector, monitor, guide throughout the star person's lifetime on planet Earth in the pre-Change Point era. 4) The Special One will be the bridge between the star person and the home dimension as the star person returns home at the Change Point 5) The Cycle is complete. The Special One is once again as he or she was in the #1 phase.

DIANE: EARTH CHANGES

Any intelligent person is very worried about planet Earth at this time. The End could come tonight, tomorrow, next week. Never before have we had the killing capabilities that we do today; the "overkill" factor is staggering! Not only can the human race kill all life on planet Earth for billions of years, but it can overkill all life on this planet many, many times over!

Remember also that the unleashing of nuclear radiation will affect not only this world but worlds/dimensions/planets which share intersect points with this one (an infinite number!). Nuclear radiation warps, destroys energy/life itself. What happens to the very soul itself which is caught in a nuclear holocaust (or even a smaller nuclear "mishap" like the meltdown of a nuclear reactor?). Is the soul damaged or destroyed? What does this mean to, for instance, the spirit world?

All star missions of all star people are aimed at the point in time when the choice will be made between life and death on planet Earth. The foremost mission (overall) is to help raise the frequency so that a new, higher dimension may be entered *without* nuclear destruction! This *is* possible, even now. If this cannot be achieved, we will work for a brave new start after limited destruction occurs.

And if there is full scale destruction, we will join hands with our Special Ones and co-workers on the home side in an attempt to salvage some life from the once beautiful Earth...to nurture it far from Earth, and to help it flourish once again.

The point is, we are as ready as we can be. Through our self-explorations as flowering star people, we are not only aware of the home dimension, but we love it and long to return to it. We also know Mother Earth well and would do all in our power to save her. We abide in Christ Consciousness, the home frequency, having not compromised to the colder, crueler materialistic dimension in which we live this human lifetime. As Tibus has stated, there are alternate time lines, alternate eddies and currents in the river Time. We must never assume that the End Days are a foregone conclusion and simply wash our hands of the whole matter, choosing not to champion rights, environmental causes, or nuclear awareness causes. We can make the future positive, it need not happen!! It may be *your* individual belief in this which will engineer Earth's reality/timeline away from nuclear destruction.

If "it" does happen, either limited or full scale, we are as ready as we can
be!

MESSAGE FROM TIBUS

This is Tibus. I come to you in Love and Light.

One thing is certain: a change in frequency/dimension will occur for planet Earth. It is simply a case of change or perish!

Our star people are living human lifetimes during this time phase for exactly that reason: to assist Earth through this Change

Point.

The "radio station", the point on the dial, *must* be changed! A new frequency of Light and Love *must* be received!

I stress that this does not mean that Earth cannot go forward in technological ways as well, cannot travel to the Future Human Consciousness in proud silver starships. In no way does the Change Point mean that Earth will become a place where "angels tread." Our star people who hail from the angelic realms will return there...but Earth herself will go on her own path at her own rate of speed...toward The Future.

The nuclear cloud hangs heavy, but rest assured that there is a silver lining. If the nuclear catastrophe occurs (and it will in some time line), then from these ashes will rise a brave new phoenix called Future Humanity. We will still take our place as valuable beings within the universe, but the path will be much harder. We hope to avert nuclear disaster in the dimension/timeline in which you find yourself.

And so, the means by which the Change Point occurs is not the main issue here (though one of grave concern). The main issue is that a new wave length of energy called the Change Point will "flood" the mundane dimension. This new energy/wavelength will seem as a tidal wave at first, particularly to those who are not flexible, adaptable and who are not familiar with star nature and spirituality. At first, it will be a "sink or swim" proposition for each essence/ soul/mind.

Once the time of turbulence is over, a new, higher dimension will dominate and will become the "home dimension" for all souls formerly of the mundane dimension. Our star people will assist those who are not familiar with the new, higher energy...for our star people have worked with it all their human lives, and it is indeed *their* wavelength, their home *energy'..*

In this way, our star people are the bridges between dimensions. They are as electrical adapters which take one wavelength of energy and translate it into another wavelength. They are special...more special than they have yet imagined!

They will lead you in the evacuation of planet Earth when and if that becomes necessary!

DIANE: RESPONSIBILITY OF A STAR SEED

There are many goals and truths which *all* of us have in common, be we defined as star people or as humans seeking enlightenment and a new path for our planet.

None of us wants nuclear war. None of us wants to pollute or kill nature. None of us wants to hurt another human nor another living being. We all seek spiritual fulfillment and a raising of consciousness level.

The star person has an added spark to this universal goal because there is a *direct link* to a higher world. Many souls follow the "regular" evolutionary paths of a planet in terms of karmic development and the soul's progression. The star person's soul comes from *outside* the regular soul development as it unfolds on this (or any) planet. The star person is a volunteer soul who did not have to follow the karmic progression but who chose to, in order to help.

Never does a star person brag about this fact. And never do we claim that there are not many, many souls from outside the regular karmic path now living, working, helping, on planet Earth...for there are!

Being a star person brings responsibility. It is not enough to earn a living and to not participate much in the cruelties of the mundane dimension. We have a responsibility to play a more active role!

Currently, one does not go down the street telling people that you are from another world. However, the day will come soon when we will be sought out to explain what is happening (at the Change Point), when we will be pressed into duty, when we will have to be the best we can be.

Many of us have great healing abilities. Other of us have the ability to be brave in the face of the unknown, to actually feel that it is our friend. There will be much bravery and courage needed! Many of us will be the psychologi cal healers of traumatized minds, others will have the ability to lead into the New Age (past the Change Point) for we are experts in it through our quiet studies and experiences! The star people movement will come out of the closet soon. It is an idea whose time has come, a people who will pave the way for a New Humanity. We will be proud to be humans...and thrilled to go out into the galaxy, to traverse dimensions, to explore new worlds...and meet the life which is out there, learning from it, offering a helping hand if necessary (just as is being done for us at this time).

The future is ours.

This is Tibus. I come to you in Love and Light.

I do not channel pages and pages on the Change Point to Diane for this is not for me to "dictate." Each reader must comprehend its significance for his or her self and meditate/think/feeL.that which I communicate. Details are not necessary and are detrimental in many ways. If I could fully communicate through human words the enormity and the significance of the Change Point which lies ahead, I would be very tempted to do so. However, it is for each of you to internalize and fully comprehend.

In conclusion I transmit to you that our star people are among you now in greater numbers than at *any* time in human history (even Biblical times).

They are among you in order to guide you through the Change Point into a new, higher dimension/world which has *not* the shallowness, the emphasis on money, nor the brutality of the current consciousness.

Some of you who are reading this know already that you are indeed star people. Diane, myself, and others have confirmed this to you but indeed you have always known it within your heart and your memory echoes.

Some of you reading this *suspect* yourself to be a star person. Do not ever underestimate yourself, do not be humble in pursuing this possibility to its fullest. Follow your inner feelings more than any overt UFO contact (or lack of it). The details of your star path (such as UFO contact or the lack of it) will become clear as your path continues.

Some of you reading this are educating yourself as to the existence of star people. We urge you to be the best humanity has to offer. One can simply raise his or her awareness level to such a point as to be on the higher frequency. This is within reach of all intelligent (sentient) life.

Our star people are among you now! Yes, they are aliens in the literal sense of the word....but they are also humans. They have lived lifetimes as human, have been initiated into human ways in painful learning experiences. They stand ready to help Earth through the Change Point just as they did when they accepted their star mission in their parallel life among us. Theirs is a love...a universal love...which transcends dimension. Theirs is a mission which abounds in the unconditional joy of helping an entire world/dimension through the most challenging and dangerous time in its history. Please love them as much as we do, we who are their co-workers of the home dimension, and search your inner being for the highest of star/spiritual qualities...for this will be your *home* frequency as well in a very short time!

11

MESSAGES FROM TIBUS

PART ONE

TIBUS CHANNELS REGARDING REINCARNATION

March 1987

I would like to use this channeling to discuss certain aspects of reincarnation with you; but before I begin, I would just like to remind you that the negativity which has been so prevalent recently is not a permanent aspect of your life. Rather, it is my opinion that much of this negativity has come into Earth's sphere because of a current "downward trend" - politically, technologically, and spiritually.

To explain, let me simply say that the star person such as yourself is sensitive to any and all changes in the Earth's magnetic fields - and those fields are, of course, comprised of living energy as well as of static energy. At any rate, it is interesting to note that your world has recently found itself in the grips of many problems - the Iran hostage situation, the continued trouble in the Middle East, the loss of the Challenger over a year ago, and a series of other, perhaps smaller problems which have all contributed to the general sense of *negativity* which has been affecting your world lately.

What is important for you to remember is that you can overcome this negativity by simply refusing to participate in it. While it isn't always possible to escape it or its influences completely, it is *always* possible to use your own spiritual awareness in order to side-step any personal involvement with it. In other words, by being aware of this negativity and by being even further aware of its cause, you gain the ability to view the situation from a much higher standpoint - that is, you develop the ability to understand the negativity, the depression which seems so common in the general populace recently, and the feeling of hopelessness which some star people have mentioned recently. As always, the key to defeating this negative energy is through your own awareness. With that awareness, you then gain the option of not participating and/or contributing to the negativity. And, of course, as energy is taken away from this negativity little-by-little, the negativity will slowly dissipate and even tually be gone. Add to your nightly meditations a mantra for harmony and well-being - for yourself, for your planet, and for all creatures with whom you share your world.

Additionally, awareness is what this reading is all about - your awareness not only of situations and circumstances in this Earthly incarnation, but awareness of previous - and even *future* - incarnations as well.

As Diane has mentioned many times previously, most people on your planet today have lived a variety of previous lifetimes - some in Rome, some in England, perhaps even some in Atlantis, Lemuria, or other so-called "mythical" societies. Wherever you lived, it is important to know that *you have* lived, and that you will live again even after passing through this current lifetime.

Many non-believers in the phenomena of reincarnation would attempt to tell us that past lives cannot be verified except under the questionable process of hypnosis. And yet, I transmit to you at this time, that such is simply not the case. Any person who truly wishes to gain an awareness of his/her previous incarnations can easily do so - through meditation and, surprisingly enough, through simple psychic/spiritual awareness.

Many times, you have undoubtedly experienced the sensation of *deja vu*
-          a feeling of "I've done this before." As I have mentioned in previous channelings, the deja vu phenomena is a very

important one to the star person as a means of comprehending the nature of time travel. But it is equally as important in developing an awareness of previous lifetimes. The feeling of "I've done this before" is one which scientists cannot accurately explain anymore than those same scientists could explain the theory of reincarnation. And yet, it is a relatively simple phenomena - one which everyone (even "un psychic" individuals) has experienced at some time in their life.

Since I have discussed the deja vu experience many times in the past, I will not use it extensively here; yet I wanted to you to be aware that it is one more way that we can begin to verify previous lifetimes. For example, when passing through a certain area of the world where you have never visited before, you suddenly know *exactly* what lies around the next bend. Perhaps this is not because your mind "races ahead of itself" as scientists would attempt to have you believe, but because, in a former existence, you travelled that same road -- whether the road was a freeway, a horse trail or nothing more than a rabbit path through dense undergrowth. Perhaps you seem to be born with certain knowledge because you *have* been here before, or because you were *drawn back* to that location *because* of a former incarnation.

For instance, the succession of individual lifetimes is no accident, no simple matter of coincidence. Each lifetime is part of a natural progression - yet each individual lifetime need *not follow* the one which, logically, should have happened *just before.* To explain, please bear with me.

It is entirely possible - even likely - that you have lived just as many *future* incarnations as *past* lives. And yet, since the human mind can only comprehend time as a linear flow of events, spiritualists, astrologers and psychics tend to refer to these other lifetimes as "past lives" for the matter of clarity. In other words, chances are that you have lived at least one lifetime in the past - perhaps in the Old West, or perhaps during the time of Queen Elizabeth I. But it is equally as likely that you have lived in the year 2010, for example, or in the year 21,110, for that matter.

In short, we are capable of skipping around in our lifetimes - for several very good reasons. Essentially, there are many lessons to be learned in each different time period, and it is often necessary that we learn a lesson which can *only* be taught in the year 2010, for example, before we can complete our "life's mission" in our lifetime in the year 1900.

For example, perhaps you have never considered that the technology your world is utilizing today is a gift *from* the future rather than a progression *toward* the future. In other words, it is conceivable that you lived a life in the year 2500 A.D., for example, and that during that lifetime you studied spaceflight extensively - for the express purpose of coming *back* to live a lifetime in the year 1995 A.D., and bring the *future* "lesson" back to the past. In short, this is called "circular lives" - and it is the only theory which can adequately explain leaps in technology, the raising of spiritual awareness, and so on.

As an easier example, consider that women, Blacks, and other "minorities" have only recently been gaining rights which have always been available to White Anglo-Saxon Protestant men. Could this be because someone who had lived in an *ideal* future society - either on Earth or on another world - came *back* to live in the early 1900's, for example, and "brought back" her knowledge of a society where men and women were equal? The same theory works quite well for any other minority. Perhaps a black man was born in the year 2200 A.D., and was able to live as an equal brother to the white man, the Oriental, the Hispanic and so on. And yet, that black man, being aware that his forebearers lived in slavery, was compelled to enter a "past life" in order to start the wheels of freedom in motion.

And, of course, there are the lifetimes we have lived on other worlds - also for the sake of learning - both for one's own individual spirit, and for the sake of bringing that acquired knowledge into whatever new lifetime he/she enters after death. The majority of all star people have lived at least one other lifetime on a world other than Earth - which often leads to the feeling of "I want to go home," or which contributes to the sensation of loneliness or "awe" which can overtake you when you look at the stars. This sense of homesickness is, of course, the result of having lived elsewhere - and the pull of your immortal spirit to return to that home which exists in the far reaches of space.

At any rate, whatever lifetimes you have lived and wherever you have lived them, the most important thing is for you to develop your awareness of these lifetimes more fully. This is critical to the star person, for it will enable you to more fully comprehend your sense of personal direction and, additionally, it will help you to more fully understand the nature of your cosmic mission. Each soul has two specific purposes in each lifetime: (1) To add to your spiritual knowledge on a personal level and; (2) To advance your cosmic mission on toward its eventual completion. Your personal spiritual development, of course, is equally as important, yet you should know that each individual lifetime furthers you on a vast, cosmic mission. Everyone who has lived or who ever will live does so for one *large* purpose and several *smaller* purposes - and by developing a greater awareness of your past lifetimes, you will gain a deeper understanding of both.

Finally, remember that you *are* important in the scope of things. You are an integral part of the cosmos itself, and you are here for a very important reason. As a star person, one part of your cosmic mission is to bring enlightenment to those around you, as well as to continually involve yourself in spiritual mysteries which are perhaps the *food* of your very soul. *This food* is part of your joy of living, part of *the fuel* which helps to stabilize an often "crazy" world, and which keeps your own spirit afloat.

Remember that we are with you, and that we will be together always. Through the common bond of other lifetimes, we have all been drawn together in this incarnation for a great purpose, and I am so very pleased to know you now, as I have known you before, and will know you again.

May the healing light of God and goodness surround you always,

Tibus.

Comment: As Tibus indicated, it is often the *unknown* (or mystery) which feeds the soul of the star person. And as long as we continue our search, I am confident that those questions will lend themselves to answers - and more questions. Additionally, as Tibus has said before, perhaps the question is of far more importance than the answer - and I now feel that I have a greater understanding of why this is so. D.M.T.

TIBUS CHANNELS REGARDING CREATIVITY, IMAGINATION AND "POETIC TRUTH."

April 1987

The creative process of thought is as valuable to them as are facts which can be learned through study. Star people are also being encouraged to utilize our creative thought processes for a variety of reasons. By using our *imagination,* it becomes possible to *see* things which otherwise might remain forever hidden. It becomes possible to speculate on the birth of a star or the death and subsequent transformation of an entire universe. It has been said that "Life itself exists within the limitless space of the mind itself." We live our solitary lives in the confines of our own head; and yet, through creative thought process, we begin to reach out - for the stars, for enlightenment, and for Ultimate Truth.

I would like to talk to you at this time about what we star guides call Poetic Truth. In essence, this is a concept which is as ancient in the Home Dimension as the concepts of life and death are here on your Earth. For the most part, the idea of Poetic Truth has not yet been "born" into your world, and through this reading, it is my hope to inspire you with the knowledge and the intuition which will give you the ability to help awaken that Truth here on your own planet.

Essentially, Poetic Truth is a combination of imagination, creativity and intuition. It begins, of course, with Intuition - one of the basic psychic gifts of the star person such as yourself.

What is Intuition? It is primarily the ability to *sense* truth or a lack of truth in something - whether it is a concept, a statement or a condition. For example, you have obviously had an opportunity to travel to some new place at some time in your life. Upon arriving at your destination, you have had *feelings* about that place - either *good* or *negative,* usually. Your Intuition tells you a sort of "history" of the place you are visiting. You *know,* for example if you are visiting a house you have never seen before, something about the people who live there. Your Intuition tells you that these are warm, loving people; or, contrapuntally, your Intuition could *warn* you that the people living in the house are *not what they seem.*

At that point, your Imagination comes into play - in the form of mental scenarios acted out on the stage of your mind. For example, if your Intuition tells you that the people living in the house you are visiting are warm and good, your Imagination encourages images of a mother and child sharing cookies and milk in the kitchen. Or, if your Intuition gives you a warning, your Imagination may well dredge up a scenario of someone having died unexpectedly in the house. You see these images on the viewscreen of your mind's eye. And, surprisingly, if you were to research the history of the house, you may well discover that your

Intuition and Imagination were "right on." Perhaps the details may have been slightly different, but in essence, your *impressions* turn out to be correct.

This is the first part of the phenomena known as Poetic Truth - the ability of the star person to combine Intuition and Imagination in order to garner a certain *truth* about people, inanimate objects or physical, geographical locations on a map. You know intuitively if you should or shouldn't travel into the desert, for example. You know intuitively that you are going to like your new boss or your new employee. And with the added dimension of your imagination, you begin to project your own *imprint* into the situation - which is where the third ingredient of Creativity comes into the picture.

All creatures are capable of Intuition and Imagination. But Creativity is an artform reserved for a select few - including star people such as yourself. Creativity is exactly what the word implies - the ability to create, to form and mold reality in accordance with your own wishes and desires. In essence, Reality Engineering is something all creatures do to one extent or another - but Reality Engineering is not exactly the same thing as employing your Creativity. You engineer your reality through unconscious actions - such as walking down one side of the street as opposed to the other, for example, or having vegetables for dinner as opposed to fruit. These more-or-less "subliminal decisions" are, of course, vitally important to your personal destiny, yet they do not employ your Creative ability to its fullest extent.

Which brings us, of course, to the concept of Poetic Truth. Poetic truth is, in a very simple explanation, the ability to combine Intuition, Imagination and Creativity in order not only to *bend* destiny, but actually to *create* it. It has often been said that everything which has been thought of now exists on some physically real plane. For example, far-flung star civilizations exist because writers have "created" them on paper and have subsequently made their writing available for others to read. Upon reading those works, others become involved in the creation/maintenance of that one writer's original "universe." A good example of this would come with a very popular television program known as *Star Trek*. It began in the mind of one writer, yet now it is a part of world culture. Everyone has heard the phrase, "Beam me up, Scotty," and almost everyone has some basic knowledge of the journeys of the USS Enterprise. And I transmit to you at this time that this is no accident. Essentially, every reality begins in the mind of one entity. The Divine Creator *thought* of the universe, and now the universe does, in fact, exist. The first man thought of his aloneness and longed for another such as himself. And now two sexes exist. Man thought of flying, and eventually air travel came into being. The list is, as you can see, endless. And it applies very strongly to the star person. Why? Because everything must first be *conceived* before it can exist. As a star person you can conceive of things far beyond the ken of most people living on your planet today. You can conceive of far-flung stars supporting peaceful civilizations. You can conceive of star-flight capability which would bring the stars within the reach of your world today. You can conceive of world peace and the harmony of Man and Animal.

And in your conception, you will learn to employ the art of Poetic Truth. In essence, by utilizing the full potential of Imagination, Intuition and Creativity, you will begin to spark the flame of realization in the minds of others. For example, it's one thing to say, "I *believe* that man will eventually go to the stars." It's another matter entirely to say, "I *know* man will eventually go to the stars."

Belief is a matter of choice. I might "believe" that the moon is made of green cheese, yet that does not make it so. But if I *know* the moon is made of green cheese, if I truly *know* it as a matter of Truth, then in some reality, the moon *is* made of green cheese. Of course, in *this* reality, the moon is the moon — composed of rock and soil and the other elements. Why? Because the majority of people know that the moon is, in fact, a physically real body just as your Earth is a physically real body.

But you can see the possibilities that this opens. If the majority of people on your Earth began to believe that the moon was made of green cheese, is it possible that the chemical structure could be changed? This is, of course, a crude example, yet it illustrates what we mean by Poetic Truth.

Existence begins with Knowledge - and Knowledge leads, eventually, to Truth. There would be no logical reason why people would *want* to believe the moon is made of green cheese, yet there is every conceivable reason why Mankind would want - *need* - to believe that your people will eventually travel to the stars and beyond. And as a star person, part of your important earthly mission is to *inspire* that need/belief/knowledge in the minds of your fellow Man.

In your heart, you certainly know that life exists on planets other than Earth. And though this is a simple concept to you, you must understand that the majority of your fellow humans never even bother to consider this idea. Through your Intuition, you know that you are not alone in this vast universe. Through your imagination, you can *see* how life might be lived on some other world. And through your Creativity, you are *charged* with the task of inspiring that absolute *knowledge* within others.

The next time you are talking to someone of the mundane dimension, you might casually ask, "What do you think about the possibility of life on other planets?" I think you'd be surprised at the answer. Some people will say they aren't interested. Others will become very uncomfortable at the question. But the majority will show some type of interest. And as you begin talking, you will start to realize that these mundane souls are actually inspired by your enthusiasm, by your absolute knowledge that you are not alone.

This is only one manner in which Poetic Truth works. It is, for the most part, a matter of *knowing* something within your own mind - and not only knowing, but *accepting* what you know as Truth. Your Intuition gives you the ability to *sense* that Truth. Your imagination gives you details of how that Truth functions. And your Creativity enables you to give a spark of your star nature to others. Also, your Creativity allows you to more accurately *see* one of those far-flung worlds, and to know the people and cultures existing on that world. Open yourself to your Creativity, my star friend, and it is my heartfelt belief that you will find another part of your own personal Answer.

We encourage you to meditate further on this concept, and to contemplate the three ingredients of Poetic Truth in conjunction. Remember that Intuition, Imagination and Creativity are all a part of the process of creation of any reality.

"To exist is to be perceived." We perceive you, my star friend, just as you perceive us. And this is, of course, only the tip of the iceberg. There is an infinite universe waiting to be explored - and that exploration must begin with a thought.

May the healing light of God and goodness surround you always,

Tibus.

Comment: Sometimes, it's easy for us to overlook our creative nature in our haste to survive and succeed in the mundane world. And yet, as Tibus has pointed out, only through the combination of Intuition, Imagination and Creativity can we hope to achieve the goals we all *perceive.* It must be through the development of spirituality *combined* with the instinct for survival that we continue our trek toward Oneness with the Cosmos, with Nature, and with our own human/star nature. D.M.T.

TIBUS CHANNELS REGARDING "BELIEF" AND

"KNOWLEDGE" May 1987

I would like to cover several topics with you at this time - most of them being of a somewhat ethereal and contemplative nature. Many times during one's day to day existence, there is a tendency to overlook the greater mysteries of Life itself; and only by allowing one's mind the freedom for that contemplation do we live up to our full potential as spiritual beings.

Meditation is perhaps one of the most critical aspects of a star person's life - not only the formalized meditation which requires silence, solitude and focus, but the more obscure forms of meditation which occur spontaneously. When you are alone with Nature, for example, or when your mind simply begins to drift as you are working, are also forms of meditation - the type which happens naturally whenever your mind feels a need to momentarily escape from the trials and tribulations surrounding you in your environment.

Which brings us to the point of personal survival in a troubled world. One of the first steps toward insuring the survival of your own serenity is to make a commitment to meditation, to remember at all times that your Mind and Spirit are of far greater importance than the self-serving needs of the Body. And while we strongly stress attention to physical needs as well, those needs can best be served when the Mind and Spirit are fulfilled and at rest.

Additionally, through your meditations, we encourage you to remember that the peace of the world begins in *your* thoughts, *in your* heart and mind. Remember that all thoughts and ideas are a form of energy - and that when you project or internalize those energies, they become forever a part of the unique fields surrounding this planet and all her people. Since you are obviously aware of the specifics, I will not go into further detail at this time, except to say that it is important to remember to project a calm, centered attitude at all times, to overcome the more base emotions of anger, possessiveness, jealousy and fear, and to subsequently replace those feelings with love, warmth and a spirit of sharing. Remember, my star friend, you are a part of this planet, too, and the energy of your thoughts and desires is an important part of the Whole. If the first step toward peace begins with a thought, then let that first thought begin within the serenity of you.

On another subject, perhaps not too closely related, I would like to discuss with you the abstract concepts of Belief and Knowledge, and how these two divergent ideas mesh with your own intuition to influence not only your own life, but the lives of those around you.

At some point in your life, you have probably encountered the universal riddle which asks: If a tree falls in the forest, but no one is present to hear it, does the falling tree make a sound?

On the surface, this may appear to be a somewhat "silly" pursuit. And yet, when we consider it in a broader perspective, it becomes possible to realize that there is no single definitive answer. For example, science *tells* us that the physics of the falling tree are not altered regardless of whether anyone is there to confirm them or not. Theoretically, the tree *does* make the same sound it would make in the presence of hundreds of people. We *believe,* because of what we are *told,* that the tree falls and an answering crash resounds through the forest. But, I ask you at this time, do *you* personally *know* this to be true? Can you, without a doubt, say with absolute *Knowledge*, that the tree falling in a deserted forest made any sound at all? Can you *know* that physics work the same without the presence of human beings to confirm them? Or are you left to wonder if indeed there are still mysteries beyond human ken?

Of course, the example of the tree and the forest is somewhat extreme, yet we star guides feel that this riddle adequately demonstrates the difference between Belief and Knowledge. Only through personal experience can one be imbued with Knowledge, thus it is critical for the star person such as yourself to continue to amass a variety of experiences, to explore the mysteries which surround you, and to inevitably draw your own conclusions based on what you know to be true. At no time should the star person simply *follow* blindly. Instead, it is within your Earthly mission to continually question, to analyze what you have been told, what you have come to *believe,* and to subsequently apply all aspects of your Whole Self as you search for your personal answers as well as for Cosmic Truths.

Mainly, the star person such as yourself is encouraged to learn the difference between a fleeting *belief* and the absolute certainty and power of Knowledge itself. For example, no matter how much we may want to *believe* that this world will eventually find peace with itself, we cannot *know* that until that Knowledge becomes a part of our personal experience. And for that reason, it becomes imperative that you do amass the experiences and the Knowledge which will enable you to *know* rather than to simply *believe.*

Secondly, I ask you at this time to contemplate the proverb of the butterfly and the man. Many years ago, a man fell asleep and dreamt he was a butterfly. Then, upon awakening, he was no longer certain whether he was a man who had dreamt he was a butterfly, or a butterfly who now dreamed he was a man.

Again, this is illustrated in rather simplistic terms, yet it is our hope that the hidden complexities will encourage you to apply this type of thinking to your daily life. At some time, you have undoubtedly said, "This can't be happening to me. It's all just a bad dream from which I'll wake up in the morning." Or, in direct opposition, you may have had a profoundly beautiful experience at some time, at which point you said to yourself: "If this is a dream, I hope never to awaken."

And while we cannot live our entire lives by such a philosophy, it is occasionally enlightening to step back and ask ourselves, "What *if* what happens today is a dream?" By doing so, it becomes possible to visualize how an alternate path might have led to a different outcome, and how embarking on that different path might *still* affect the balance of the situation. For example, let us assume that a man is fired from his job and that, after the fact, he steps back with the attitude that the entire incident was nothing more than a bad dream. By gaining the perspective of distance, by sometimes telling yourself that daily experiences are of no more *consequence* than a simple dream, it becomes possible to gain a greater understanding of one's place within the Cosmic structure of the Universe itself. By realizing that no job is permanent, by understanding that even the nature of the most loving relationship is subject to change (positive or negative), we begin to realize that all we have been led to *believe* throughout our lives is really insignificant when compared to the majesty and scope of the infinite universe. By accepting that our lives are perhaps nothing more than a dream in the mind of God, we begin to understand that our primary function in each individual lifetime is to learn, to amass experiences through which we gain a deeper comprehension of our function and our goals.

Of course, these same philosophies can be narrowed down to a more personal field at any time. Rather than viewing the subject on a Cosmic level, it is possible to view the same circumstances on a day-to-day level as well. Then, as you begin to realize both the significance and the *in* significance of the mundane world, your mind will automatically seek the serenity to be found on higher, more spiritual levels. By abandoning *beliefs* for the pursuit of *Knowledge,* the star person such as yourself is filled with understanding, serenity and ultimate harmony with oneself and with the greater universe.

Finally, remember that the path to Knowledge and Awareness is never an easy road to follow. It is a path which requires commitment, dedication and perseverance. And yet, I transmit to you at this time that the rewards of following this path will far outweigh the obstacles and even the occasional pain which is a part of any genuine desire to accomplish a new task.

Remember that what you *believe* to be true may be nothing more than an illusion, a concept which is shattered under the light of scrutiny and personal examination. But what you *know* to be true - *those* truths which resound in your heart and fly free in your spirit - those are the eternal truths which will bring peace in times of trouble, serenity in times of turmoil. And it is those truths which will see you safely Home to the stars and finally beyond.

May the healing light of God and goodness surround you always,

Tibus

Comment: I realize that many of these concepts are perhaps strange and unusual, yet it is Tibus' desire that you should continue to ponder the mysteries of Life as well as those safe paths which we all tend to choose at times. Only when we abandon the "safe and easy" path for the spiritual pursuits of enlightenment and awareness will we achieve Balance within ourselves, and with the Cosmos as well.

When we remember that the Star Person *chose* this lifetime and this Earthly mission, we begin to understand that we are here for a very important reason, and that only by applying ourselves with full *Knowledge* will we be able to defeat the laziness which accompanies a simple "belief system." We must *know* that we *are]* only then can we truly *be.* D.M.T.

TIBUS CHANNELS REGARDING "THE BALANCE" YIN AND YANG WORKING TOGETHER TO CREATE A BETTER, MORE PERFECT WORLD. July 1987

This is a time of great energy on your planet - some positive, some negative. But what is important is that you avail yourself of *all* aspects of this energy. The positive energy can, of course, be utilized in your daily life, through meditation, enlightenment and your own growing awareness. Negative energy, on the other hand, cannot be ignored either, and must *first* be incorporated into the *positive* energy before it can be of positive benefit to anyone or anything.

Briefly, it is possible to work with negative energy in two ways. The first method is simply to make a conscious effort to dispel negative energy through the positive powers of meditation, prayer and creative visualization. To do this, one needs only visualize a void of darkness being penetrated by the pure goodness of the White Light of Healing. This seems simple, but it does indeed work - particularly if you can visualize the healing light surrounding and eventually *absorbing* all negativity until only goodness remains.

The second method of ridding oneself (or one's planet) of negative energy is to make a conscious attempt to turn the negative energy into positive. For example, a rainstorm is viewed by many people as being a negative thing, i.e., it may serve to ruin a planned picnic or outing to the beach. But on the other hand, when one attempts to see that the rainstorm is necessary to cleanse the planet, nourish the trees, and breathe Life into a desert (for example), one begins to see that what one initially viewed as a *negative* aspect is, in fact, a very *positive* aspect instead.

Additionally, try to visualize the same "void" of darkness as described above. But instead of visualizing the White Light of Healing *absorbing* that darkness, try to imagine what might happen if that "void" was simply turned wrong-side-out. Since it is a universal constant that all things have their opposite (love/hate, light/dark, slavery/freedom, etc.), it is certainly true that positive and negative are also two sides of the same coin. Thus, instead of visualizing that negativity becomes absorbed by light, focus your meditations on the possibility of light and darkness working together.

As you know, your planet is highly dependent on cycles of day and night (light and dark). Typically, the night has been viewed by certain religious sects as being "evil" or "negative." But, like the rainstorm, periods of Earth- darkness are necessary in order to preserve life on your planet. For example, consider what would happen if there was no nighttime. Your world would exist in a perpetual state of sunlight — which would eventually cause the trees to perish, the nocturnal animals (such as bobcats, coyotes, owls and other species) to become extinct. On the other hand, a state of perpetual darkness would destroy the trees just as quickly because of the lack of light to complete the chlorophyll cycle. Many human beings would suffer irreparable psychological harm , and your planet would, again, be plunged into a state of chaos.

I use these examples primarily to illustrate that all things must work together in harmony and balance in order for Life itself to flourish. This is equally as true of positive and negative energy. Consider your planet as a gigantic battery - and, as with any battery, it must have a positive charge and a negative (grounding) charge. Without the ground of negativity, the battery would not function. And without the positive spark to ignite the flame, the planet would remain grounded in utter negativity.

Please understand, my friend, that we starguides are not advocating the *use* of negativity to attain personal goals or long-term desires. Rather, we are pointing out that each aspect always has its opposite. Death is the temporary resting place after life. Life is how we begin anew after physical death. This is true for the spirit as well as the flesh - and although the spirit itself can never truly "die," it does go through periods of dormancy (or rest/hibernation) before embarking on its next physical incarnation. This is part of the spirit Life Cycle, and a part which we encourage the star person such as yourself to meditate upon whenever possible.

Aside from the subject of positivity and negativity, another concept I would ask you to consider at this time is this: What is the sound of one hand?

In ancient times, the Zen religion asked this question of many pupils - to meditate upon the sound of one hand clapping. Now, we as your star guides pose this same question to you, in the hopes that your meditation will lead you to discover that the universe holds little of "logic" in its sphere.

Additionally, as you ponder this concept (the sound of one hand clapping), we ask you to consider the topic of silence itself. What *is* silence? At any time, anywhere on your Earth, there is some sound - either that of the wind or a stream, traffic or the shouts of children at play.

In the mind, however, silence can and should dwell - as a form of meditative serenity, and as a retreat to which the star person such as yourself can flee from the constant turmoil of the mundane (Earthly) world. Only when the mind embraces silence can full awareness be achieved - and only in the mind can full silence be discovered. This is not simply a matter of meditation to achieve silence. Rather, it is a matter of putting the mind, body and spirit in balance - and allowing the spirit to lead the mind and body into the silent places where true awareness begins.

This is an exercise which should be done on occasion, though one which should not be overdone - for the simple reason that the conscious mind requires the noise of Life in which to complete its mundane journey. However, when the star person such as yourself can begin to gain control over that conscious mind, thereby allowing the *subconscious* mind its "freedom" as well, a giant step toward spiritual freedom has been taken.

It is our belief that the Silence of Spirit Meditation will enable you to more fully understand the chaos which surrounds you in your mundane (Earthly) life, and to gain a greater ability to cope with the negativity which often invades one's day to day existence. Remember that chaos and negativity are natural states of existence in this universe - just as spirituality and serenity are natural states as well (all things in balance). In order to understand one, a commitment must be made to understand all. Only in this manner will true awareness be achieved.

Finally, as you begin these simple exercises, I advise you to seek the counsel of your Special One. The star person, as you well know, is served by an individual star guardian (just as I serve Diane). It is this "bonding" between the Earth-spirit (the star person) and the Cosmic Spirit (your Special One) that allow both parties to learn from one another and to grow in a mutually beneficial direction. Remember also that we star guides seek to learn from *you* just as you seek to learn from *us* - a balanced goal which will have much greater rewards than a more typically one-sided venture.

As you conduct your daily meditations, call upon your Special One to guide you toward the Silence of Mind - the condition of non-thinking wherein the Whole Spirit is allowed its freedom, thereby allowing you a deeper sense of awareness and enlightenment. There is perhaps no deeper commitment than that between the star person and the Special One, and though we may not stress this aspect often enough, it is profoundly true.

Remember always that you are unique, you are a creature of balance and harmony, a spirit on a quest for enlightenment and freedom. Purify your heart through meditation, strengthen your body through spiritual healing and the correct herbal teas which your Special One can recommend, and prepare your Spirit for the most important journey thus far.

May the healing light of God and goodness surround you always,
Tibus.

Comment: My best possible guidance for star people at this time is to ask you to remember that no path is an easy one save that which is not a path at all. In simple terms, we must commit ourselves to a goal, set for ourselves certain long-term goals. If we sit back and simply "wait" for enlightenment to come to us, it never will. It is only when we seek awareness - and make a commitment to achieve that awareness through our labors - that awareness becomes possible.

As star people, we must *always* strive to remember that all things must exist in balance - light cannot exist without darkness, hate cannot exist without love, good cannot exist without evil. Then, by striving to accept the balance of the Cosmos into our daily lives, we will be able to see that we cannot right *all* wrongs (but we *can* right a few); we cannot always feel *only* love (but we *can* make the love we *do* feel work for the betterment of Humankind); we cannot exist in a world *without* evil (but we *can* make our own goodness *count* as we let our star-light shine).

We *can* achieve this Balance - both personal and spiritual as well. It is, like any other path, a difficult one. But Knowing that it is *possible* makes it work - for ourselves, for our planet, and for all the lifeforms with whom we share this immense universe. D.M.T.

12

MESSAGES FROM TIBUS

PART TWO
TIBUS CHANNELS REGARDING SIMULTANEOUS LIVES

This is Tibus. I come to you in love and light.

Recently a question was asked regarding whether star people are also simultaneously on the ships with their star guardians.

I wish to communicate with you on this very vital and wonderful subject. First, I would like to offer a quote from Kahlil Gibran:

"All things in this creation exist within you, and all things in you exist in creation: there is no border between you and the closest things, and there is no distance between you and the farthest things and all things, from the lowest to the loftiest, from the smallest to the greatest, are within you as equal things. In one atom are found all the elements of the Earth; in one motion of the mind are found the motions of all the laws of existence; in one drip of water are found the secrets of all the endless oceans; in one aspect of you are found all the aspects of existence."

There is an inclination on the part of the human race to take matters literally, in a mundane sense - and this warps these matters beyond recogni tion of Truth. This is not a fault on the part of the human race. It is simply a phase in their "adolescent" development. Teenagers tend to seek immediate gratification, they feel they will never grow older or wiser. They live for today. This is how the human race is, at this point in their evolution. Therefore, if we transmit to our friends that they are with their star guardians simultaneously or that they are UFO occupants, or that they are at Home...we have found that this tends to translate as, "Last night I went to Venus on a spaceship," or, "I am simultaneously the high commander of the fleet."

This is why the contacts of the 1950s did not work out better as time went on. As with a child perceiving Christmas, humankind perceives one present under the tree or one light on the tree, but the concept of all that Christmas is, tends to elude the child until he is older (there are so many levels to understanding, all are equally a valid part of The Question and The Answer).

With this said, we quote our friend, Dr. Leo Sprinkle: "Us folk will become UFOLK."

It is a truth that our star people will become - and simultaneously are - we of the Home Side.

However, this is not simply a case of one aspect of a star person reaching out to another aspect of the same person...if this concept were understood as this, it could be argued that we of the Home Side are not really "out there," that UFOs are not real, that there is no higher contact...because what we would then be saying (in most of humanity's perception), would be that some "spacey" people were dreaming of the future, and that even though they were wrong in their perception that there are space intelligences, their dreams will nonetheless become catalysts toward humankind evolving spiritually and in humankind going into space one day.

Now the outcome of such dreams is a worthy one and in essence the same one as we champion; however, not I nor anyone else on the Home side is willing to concede that we are not real.

The simple truth is, that we are "out there," UFOs are real and there is higher contact!

A similar concept is that of past and future lives. In human perception, they are viewed as linear on the timeline. We find that they are more accurately perceived as "bubbles in time" and therefore, we use the term "parallel aspects of the Whole Self" in an effort to make that concept a more clear and pure one.

When the concept of our star people becoming - and being - us is purely and clearly perceived, this cements the relationship between the Special One and the star person.

We have discovered that the human race is shackled with the perception that TIME is an absolute. Reality can therefore only be viewed from a limited view. We have discovered that the greatest liberating event which can befall a race occurs at the moment that the knowledge of TIME BEING RELA TIVE enters into the mass consciousness (of that race). This cosmic revelation must happen only when a race which is spiritually ready (unconditionally loving and peaceful).

We would be wrong to simply spring this knowledge on the majority of humans that many of us are humans from the future. Yes, there are aliens here from far distant planets circling far distant suns...but that concept would not be as upsetting to the human race as the knowledge that others of us are Future Humans. However, this and other "earthshaking" knowledge will have to be made known to humanity before it is spiritually ready to know these things due to events of the Change Time/Point. We/you can only work as hard as we can beforehand to prepare humanity...

Even though star people like yourself are used to the idea that time is traversable and relative, we realize that it is still hard to truly interiorize the idea that you are us and yet that we are separate beings, real unto ourselves. In the present reality, some of us have gone to live human lifetimes (you) while others of us have stayed behind to protect and guide (us). However, in a parallel and equally valid reality, we are all here. You have made this fact a reality by your noble work in your present lifetime. You have created a path home for yourselves and for all Earth.

As you can see, these concepts become confusing and nonsensical to one who has not achieved a certain level of awareness. Therefore, we do not approach this subject directly with all people. The worst that can happen is that the person declares that he himself flies to Venus in starships when no one else does or that he, himself is, in a parallel aspect, high commander of the fleet when no one else is. This is a perception which has the human ego very much involved in it. This is not wrong, it is merely a stage of adolescence, but it can lead down a false path.

We await you along the *true* star path!

May the healing light of goodness surround you, always,
Tibus
TIBUS CHANNELS REGARDING SENSITIVES

In a meditative session, Diane asked Tibus, " My dreams, like those of others, are very interesting and I've often thought that they are memories of mine from some past/future life or that they are perhaps are they your memories. Just what are they? I am especially inclined to actually remember what a starship is like, feel I belong there. I'm not alone in this starship feeling, of course, as a good many star people have it (and even some science fiction fans if they would admit it). Tibus, can you give me a "more official" answer (I don't have one at all, actually. I just know this strange memory/feeling exists)? Sometimes it's like I am watching a sequence like an old newsreel."

This is Tibus. I come to you in Love and light.

Sensitives have "memories" which are ingrained in their beings - in their hearts and souls - but are not readily accessible as memories in their physical brains. Now, by "sensitives" I realize I am using an old term, one used by the Spiritualist movement many years ago. This does not add or detract from its usage, I am merely reminding you that this term has been used before. I find that, as I channel through to Diane, there is no other word in her repertoire of English which can be used in this concept. If we said that *psychics* have memories which are ingrained in their hearts and souls, the earthly concept conjures up "official psychics" - professionals. Again, neither a negative or positive in itself but not useful for our concept.

Star people certainly are among the group of sensitives on Earth who have these strong feelings/memories but there are many others, also, not deeply involved in space contact or star guardian "research" but still with memories. For example, the man who has always been fascinated beyond logical bounds with Ireland. He saves money to visit it, he finds a special place and the only explanation is that he lived a "haunting" past life in this place. This man is "normal" in other aspects, does not feel alienated or that he has a special mission. This man fits the status quo in most ways. I do not wish to belabor explaining why I wish to use the word "sensitives" in this transmission, but I simply find it the only accurate description.

Certainly, any student of metaphysics is a sensitive. All star people are sensitives or they would not fit the "star" description.

Now, to further complicate matters, you *do* have a link - open and natural - to your special one. Your star guardian is also certainly a "sensitive." Most universal beings are. Mundane humankind has managed to block spiritual conduits, partially with the static of mundane life which does not transcend at all, and partially with the prejudices against being "sensitive" or "psychic" which traditional Christianity has instilled. I hasten to add that Christianity is not the only offender here, nor is it an offender at all in its pure form. Many Earth religions teach their people to be blind followers of dogma and to be afraid of reaching out for themselves.

Assume you are a sensitive who picks up past and future memories which your heart and soul remember, but which are missing from your physical brain that has been with you only in this lifetime (and by "heart" we obviously mean the spiritual heart; again, English is lacking some words!). You are also a sensitive who picks up the star guardian. You do so even though sometimes these energies may seem scrambled in with your own. And, we also add that one cannot truly define what the sub/supra consciousness is as it relates to the physical brain. The sub/supra consciousness, we have found, is the bridge to the soul from the physical brain which houses the conscious mind.

It all becomes very confusing, and this is our point. We understand why it is tempting to try to find exact answers to memories of the heart and soul - you may not be able to "unblend" the blend which has occurred throughout the ages. The unique energy which is *you* has been touched - loved, hated, and all emotions in between - by other energies (other individuals). In this way, even they are blended into your being, for their love, for instance, has made a difference in some pathway you have taken along the line. Certainly your star guardian/cosmic soulmate has made this difference many times and has blended well with *you.*

In a recent transmission, we mentioned that the star guardians would be letting our Star People know about other aspect(s) we have lived, some not as "exalted" as our current status (for we have had no free passes up the ladder; we have learned through long, hard lessons just as all souls). How can this incoming information be separated from what you might interpret as your own past life experience? Ah, there is that question again of unblending an age-old blend. It is difficult, and sometimes we feel it is not necessary. Other times, it is necessary if a particular lesson must be realized by one soul alone.

Our star people sometimes remind us of children searching for their hidden Christmas presents. If the children stopped to think, perhaps they would not want to know what the present is *before* Christmas morning; they also might realize that scouting out the hiding place was not the object of Christmas giving, and this scouting out is bothersome to their parents. Now, once again, I am not aiming to be patronizing or condescending in my analogies nor do I mean that our star people are ever bothersome to us! I simply mean that to find the specific present (past life or specific source of a transmission or memory) *before* the time it is to be made known naturally, through events of the cosmos, may not be the most important part of your star path. Yet, it is tempting. The world trains one to find answers to all questions. Mundane earth does not teach the child to treasure the *question.*

Sensitives can feel the currents of the Cosmos. This perhaps further complicates matters in deciding exactly where certain memories/feelings are coming from, but remember that regardless of which alternate path is taken, the star path is continued upon, as long as you are of *goodness,* as long as you remain a "sensitive," as long as you *care* about the future of planet Earth and her lifeforms - and act in some way to manifest this caring.

May the healing light of goodness surround you, always, Tibus

TIBUS CHANNELS REGARDING UNCONDITIONAL LOVE
This is Tibus. I come to you in love and light.

Love is indeed the greatest of vibrations, frequencies! Man has had little trouble in immortalizing "love" as long as it is ego based. Man loves woman. Woman loves man. There is parental love, etc. These forms of love are very beautiful (though of course humankind manages to get physical biology mixed up with LOVE, particularly in his young years. If these two can accompany each other, there is indeed a beautiful relationship formed). Man's version of LOVE is at exactly the same stage as his religion. He "channels" love through very narrow tunnels. There is conditional love, but very little UNCONDITIONAL LOVE. There is ego-centered religion, but very little tuning into the beautiful and loving Divine Energy, feeling The Flow in the magnificent never-ending Cycle.

I wish to digress a moment to say that you must not fear that your "ego" becomes too big over our spoken truths to you...and about your beautiful awareness. Your "ego" is an UNCONDITIONAL LOVE. It is not a mundane ego. It is rather a feeling of BEING, of purity, of goodness, of LIFE. It is well and good to be reminded of these lovely qualities within yourself. It is well and good to revel in them for you know them to be universal in nature. Your center is not within mundane SELF, but, rather toward the HIGHER SELF which extends lovingly toward infinity. Allow yourself to be washed in the knowledge that you have indeed reached much wisdom and beauty. Yes, of course, there is still a ways to go, as is true for all of us!

Jesus/Sananda often spoke in parables and analogies so that humankind could comprehend the UNCONDITIONAL LOVE of which he spoke. He used these methods, as we Space Brothers often do, to attempt to make man realize that ego-base is pitifully wanting in new qualities; that through symbolism, mankind might realize himself a child of the stars and the universe. Alas, man just does not seem to "get it."

Small advancement has been made. We must *teach* /reach humankind to think in parables, symbols, analogies - for starters. In this way, love will advance to UNCONDITIONAL LOVE, and ego-base will advance to cosmic awareness. Also, the Whole Mind/Soul concept says this also. It is another way of saying that man must truly revolutionize his concept of his dimension, his universe, and his mind.

Yes, the whole "experiment" of humankind on planet Earth is to set up this level of consciousness. Our craft, which were spotted in Earth skies, are to be symbols as well as physical objects. Our messages hold many symbols for humankind as well as specific truths (often, specific dates are given for mass landings of our craft because a channel goes amok in translating our transmissions within his or her mind - from symbolism into practical detail, like an Earth date). Often also, our channels run amok when they take an ego trip about being a "chosen one," totally missing the symbolism, which is the hard part of the message to get across in the first place! Oh, we have no trouble in getting a man to spot a "UFO" in the sky. However, we have great trouble in transmitting to the same man what the parable is, what the analogy is, what the symbolic message is for his mind/soul and for his entire race.

This first and foremost level is, as we have indeed realized, UNCONDITIONAL LOVE and a lessening of ego-base, to a far greater degree than humankind has in the latter part of the Twentieth Century. We are, first and foremost, ambassadors of this love to planet Earth. This is our cosmic mission.

The second Level is that we are physical beings (are not all energies physical within their home dimension?) who travel the stars, who are composed of many different races from many planets, many dimensions, many timeframes. The term "alien" has been used so much in Earth movies, etc., that we hesitate to use it at all. And yet, if we do not, humankind will never be able to comprehend his encounters, meetings and ultimate blending with us. If we do not give man a "conditional" and ego-based" term (''alien"), he can never begin to get the full, Whole Mind, picture, which is not "alien" at all. Eventually humans must become of UNCONDITIONAL LOVE, of universal wisdom, of cosmic citizenship.

It is a vicious circle which we travel with humans: If we give them a term they understand, they "tag" it, build a prejudice against it, or at least a very mundane base for it, never touching on the symbolism involved, never even daring to guess the greater significance than that related to their small world/ ego. If we don't give them the "term" or concept at all it goes almost totally without "manifestation" on the Earth level.

A moment ago, I spoke to you of the *two levels* we work on. On the more important level, yes, certainly, all forms of life are fashioned in God's image...for God gives life...God is. Life is sacred, be it humanoid or vastly different from human. Life is sacred, whether it exists in a three dimensional reality or a more "alien" one.

On our second "priority" (level), I would like to give you the interesting fact that humanoid life is spread throughout this galaxy and throughout many dimensions. Humans, of course, were not the first human-like beings. Ages ago, many humanoids were seeded on various hospitable planets. Of course, this fits into the *larger scheme* (our Level One priority which perhaps should be called the spiritual level, while Level Two is the scientific level.). Though there are delightful diversities and billions of variations throughout this galaxy (we will not even begin to touch on others!), the "image of man" is a familiar one across the universe. Also, the Divine Energy which pulses through humans does form itself into a physical reality which *pleases it* - which manifests it beautifully. Humankind has much more to be proud of than he dares imagine (not in egotistical terms but in unconditional terms).

My mission is partially to tell humankind (and particularly our star people) that rather than feeling shame at being human, we must find a *new pride,* one which I would like to call unconditional pride (please interchange this term with unconditional joy). It is not ego-based. It is an essential with unconditional love.

If the child does not like/love himself, there are serious problems. He must not feel that all those he meets are *superior* to him or he will eventually act badly. He must realize his equality and have pride in this fact - but *unconditionally,* without the typical egotism entering (that is a false pride).

Finally, I would like again to stress the importance of SYMBOLS. This is a term which has been stressed so much in philosophy, and even in the occult, that one grows numb to it.

However, as in the case of Tarot cards, in the Jungian psychology findings, even the night hawks and sentient coyotes, symbols are given. We will be finding great pleasure and joy in giving you many amazing symbols in the time ahead. We realize, my friend, that you have dealt with these in wonder and joy for many years, but in the troubled times ahead, the symbols will increase in intensity and quantity.

May the healing light of goodness surround you always,
Tibus

13

MESSAGES FROM TIBUS

PART THREE
CHANNELING ON PROPHECY

This is Tibus. I come to you in love and light.

Questions to be asked in this transmission:

1. What is meant by the expression, "the gift of prophecy?"

    What is the difference between prophecy and precognition?

2. Have only a few individuals throughout human
    history been blessed with the gift of prophecy?
    Can anyone develop a talent for prophecy?

3. Why should you work on developing prophetic abilities?
    Does your star guardian (spirit guide) need your help - your
    gift of prophecy in order to guide planet Earth on a loving,
    peaceful path? How can you possibly help from the Earth
    plane?

4. Isn't our higher guidance omnipotent?
    Can't they change things from "on high" if they wish?
    Why is your gift of prophecy so important?

5. Can you be a pivotal force in stopping global nuclear war?
    Can the power of your mind and soul make a better world
    for people everywhere as well as for yourself?

121

In perceiving the question and possible answer to #1 of this transmission, we refer to the Earth studies of psychology and sociology.

As you know, the study of psychology refers to the study of one's individual emotional and mental characteristics. Incidentally, psychology is not a study which belongs to Earth alone, because throughout the universe with all its billions of sentient lifeforms (beings) - each and every one has a unique psychology. The Creator Spirit is indeed wondrous and diverse!

Now let us consider sociology. This is the study of a race of lifeforms such as the human race and its many subdivisions such as various cultures and tribal units called countries.

Psychology is to the gift of precognition as sociology is to the gift of prophecy.

In other words, if you have the gift of predicting the future of an individual, you are blessed with precognition.

If you have the gift of predicting the future of an entire race, you are blessed with the gift of prophecy.

The gift of prophecy involves the ability to step outside a planet's historical flow and to perceive with acute vision exactly where that planet is going *if* it remains on its current path.

Each and every planet has a historical flow. The flow of human events on planet earth is a pageant which flows along a timeline (a time continuum) which is capable of being perceived when one steps out of it. One may do this by removing his or her unique mind/soul from this timeline and looking at it from "on high," as if in a starship.

For instance, when we perceive Earth from "on high" at its present intersect point on the time continuum, we see that this magnificent planet is headed for global destruction. If *you* also know this, analyze your knowledge: Is it based primarily on a logical conclusion (yes, everyone knows the facts about nuclear proliferation and the polluting and contaminating forces at work presently on Earth)? Or is your knowledge based on a *feeling'*]

In other words, though you factually know that planet Earth is in trouble, does your knowledge of its possible destruction come from your logic circuits or from your heart? If the knowledge comes from your heart (and mind/soul), then yours is the gift of prophecy; and the intelligence which your logic circuits contribute tell you this as well. Yours is a twofold insight!

Earth is on a collision course. Is this course irreversible?

Is prophecy a truth which is a foregone conclusion? If this is true, we might think of prophecy as a curse rather than a gift.

However, do not despair because the collision course is reversible. That which the prophet perceives is a truth which is not a finished reality. There are always alternate paths to be taken. And how can planet Earth know that there are indeed alternate timelines? This world can and will know through your gift of prophecy!

The gift which forecasts destruction is indeed a gift - not a curse - simply because it is a tool. It is the catalyst by which alternate timelines of freedom, peace, and love can be found.

Now, if you have prophetic insight such as Jesus, Nostradamus, Muhammad, The Buddha, and many others have possessed throughout human history, and you do not use it to influence humans away from the collision course, then it is of no good to you or anyone else. Prophecy is a gift which must be used, which must speak out and be heard (or scream out, if necessary), it must influence others with all the power which any individual can put behind it! Consider the great souls mentioned in this paragraph: Did not they use their gifts of prophecy in order to guide the human race away from bigotry, greed, and destruction?

All human beings - all sentient lifeforms everywhere in the universe - have the potential for the gift of prophecy. Some never think about this gift - or feel it - and so it does not develop. Others may suspect it is there within themselves - a direct conduit to the Creator Spirit - but they do not take time and energy to develop it. Still others may be humble, feeling that they have a mystical knowledge of Earth's historical flow within themselves but that it is up to the "great prophets" to do the big time prophecy work.

The truth is, the Creator Spirit which dwells in all humans pleads with all humans to use their gift of prophecy so as to guide the lovely blue/green planet into a free, peaceful, creative future reality. The great prophets were great because they stood behind their prophecies, telling others about them. They made this a full time mission. Though modern day demands prohibit you from working twenty-four hours a day on altering earth's collision course, still it is a universal responsibility to do all you can in guiding Earth toward a positive future. If there is not a positive future, there is nothing.

In order to develop your gift of prophecy, you must step *outside* Earth's historical flow but you do so from *inside* Earth's

123

historical flow. You are a part of a timeline. To develop your gift of prophecy, you float above this timeline from which you spring - and you see the entire path of Earth throughout the ages in perspective.

You see the forest instead of the trees, but your take-off point is from within the trees.

If you understand this concept, then you will receive the question and possible answer to #3 and ultimately #4 at the beginning of this transmission.

Consider yourself and your link to your spirit guide (and we reaffirm that all beings have these loving, wise guides): You are a being who wishes freedom, peace, love, and creativity for Earth who is of Twentieth Century Earth. Oh, it is true that your mind/soul may well have origins and connections to other worlds and to the higher dimensions. However, your physical body is that of a Twentieth Century human and in many ways, your daily life is that of a being who lives in the Twentieth Century historical flow.

As a being from outside the Twentieth Century Earth flow, your spirit guide (star guardian) attempts to contact, guide, and help Earth - and particularly to help you to a path of freedom, peace, and universal brotherhood. However, your star guardian cannot openly interfere with Earth's history because each planet must determine its own destiny from inside its reality base (timeline). Each planet has its own karma and continues to make its own karma.

You are within this planet's reality base. You can help determine the destiny from inside. You are a part of Earth's karma, even though you are not entirely of Earth. You are living a lifetime as a human and therefore you have a legitimate right to influence her reality base in as active a way as you can!

In this way, your star guardian needs your help. You will work from inside to help earth away from her collision course, into a bright New Age while the guides in other dimensions work from outside with gentle protection and subtle help. You are to be the positive factor personified within Earth's present reality base. Without your work, an all-important element would be missing and the collision course will indeed flow onward to its tragic end.

You must never forget that God Consciousness dwells within you. You are not an island, either on Earth or in the universe.

Your mind/soul springs from the cosmic wellspring of eternal energy - the Creator Spirit. You have also experienced life on Earth. Considering both of these glorious facts, you cannot simply stand by and wait for other individuals to save earth from its collision course. You are vital.

In perceiving the words in this transmission, you are exercising the muscles of prophecy. In perceiving yourself as a human standing among the trees *and* as a being who looks down on the forest from "on high," you are well on your way to full use of the gift of prophecy which you possess.

Feel the throb of the historical flow around you. Immerse yourself in the drama of the intersect point on the timeline on which you now stand. *Be* a part of the reality base around you. Now...!

Rise above this reality base in a starcraft which travels the starry seas. Look down on the planet below you and perceive the flow of history which is planet Earth. Notice that the intersect point is one in billions of points in time and that this one point can be a veering off place for a *whole new timeline.*

At any point on the continuum, you may change the flow. The timeline need not head straight into oppression, misery, or total destruction.

This is the true gift of prophecy. You now have the knowledge not only of the future but you are aware that in perceiving the future, you can *change* it! *Use* your gift of prophecy because of all the spiritual/psychic gifts such as precognition, healing, psychokinesis, telepathy, and others, prophecy is the one to be used the most, for the welfare of the most lifeforms - and ultimately for your welfare as a citizen of Earth and of the Universe.

May the healing light of goodness surround you, always,

Tibus

CHANNELING ON CHANNELING

This is Tibus. I come to you in love and light.

Questions to be asked in this transmission:

1. What is the definition of channeling?

    What is the difference between channeling and mediumship, a skill which psychic spiritualists have presented to humankind for years?

2. What are the indications that a person is making contact
   with other realms of existence?
   How can a person tell when telepathic contact is being sought
   from other realms?
   What is the one thing to remember when either seeking
   contact or allowing outside contact to enter your
   mind/soul frequency?

3. How does one turn this contact into channeling or
   mediumship which will give messages of help and inspiration
   to other people as well as being positively useful to yourself?
4. What are some suggestions for enhancing/inviting contact
   with higher dimensions?

In perceiving the question and possible answer to #1, we first
look into the phenomenon of thought itself.

The human brain functions much as a sophisticated computer,
storing information and experience. But what of the nuances of
emotion, intuition, inspiration, and revelation? Was it the brain of
Beethoven which wrote the immortally beautiful music or was his
music reflective of the *spirit* and the *mind?* Was not the brain of
Beethoven designed like all other brains? Indeed, it was something
beyond the computer/brain which created his genius and his
music. The brain of Einstein has been examined and it has been
found that his brain in itself was like all other brains. There were
not unusual convolutions or patterns of grey matter in this genius'
brain. Yet, something in this man set him aside from the rest of
humanity, put him light years ahead of the rest of his species. That
something is intangible; it cannot be dissected as the brain can be.

Once you internalize this premise, we can consider the
question of channeling. First we consider how real is the spirit and
the mind but how very hard to "catch," to define, to dissect. One's
spirit - the mind/soul -lives in a physical vessel which is the
human body, for a period of years, then passes on to other worlds,
other lives. When a person channels messages, he or she is
allowing his own mind/soul to take a rest while another mind/soul
temporarily uses the brain to give a message. The brain (the
physical body) of one inhabiting the mundane dimension (daily
world), must be used by this visiting mind/soul because it is the
only way to interact in the Earth dimension. Unless a physical

126

body which is native to the mundane dimension is used, the visiting mind/soul remains in its home dimension.

When an individual channels a mind/soul from another dimension or another planet, that individual is *willingly* allowing the physical body and brain to be host to the other consciousness. This consciousness can then transmit knowledge and information which it (he or she) possesses about Twentieth Century earth. The visiting consciousness can give warnings, wisdom, and help. It can do this because it is of a *higher* consciousness frequency.

As a matter of fact, one can easily tell if one is in contact with a higher plane instead of a lower one, simply by the nature and quality of the information. If the information is petty, hateful, of base sexual nature, or totally egotistical, then it is of a lower world. If the information is encouraging, speaks of peace on Earth, good will toward men, tells of universal love and brotherhood, and tells one about the wonder of the positive way of being, then it is of a higher level.

Now, all the information which has just been given may also apply to the skill of mediumship. Spiritualists and psychics have for years been able to go into trances and give messages from the spirit world, speaking in a different voice than usual, with a difference cadence or tone. Often these mediums can give messages directly from a deceased relative or loved one. Sometimes they can give messages from famous people who have passed to other realms.

Channeling, however, deals with the sharing of the physical body (brain) with a visiting mind/soul who has not necessarily passed from the earth plane. Channeling usually deals with sharing consciousness with a being of a higher plane - from a different planet or time - who is therefore an alien. He or she has not died on mundane Earth and is thus not passing messages back to the earthly plane from the spirit world. The mind/soul who channels, therefore, usually identifies him or herself as from space or from another planet.

The brain of the medium or channel is the *common ground* between the two lifeforms. The brain of the medium is also the common ground between the human psychic and the spirit world energy. A gifted medium or channel knows how to allow his or her own mind/spirit to become calm, peaceful, and low key so that the visiting consciousness can transmit the message.

Yes, the frequencies of the two lifeforms involved must be

127

similar. A channel picks up the mind/soul waves (frequency) of a space or dimensional being because these waves are adaptable and similar to his or her own waves. Some channels have the ability to pick up many frequencies while others pick up one or two. However, often the channels who consistently pick up the same one or two frequencies do so at a greater accuracy and on a more regular schedule.

Whether the gifted person is a channel or a medium, we may say that he or she shares consciousness with another mind/soul for a while. Sometimes this is a short while, as in the case of the trance medium who cannot sustain the contact for hours. Other times, as in the case of some space contacts, the consciousness-sharing goes on continuously but is formally activated if a formal channeling is requested.

Humankind is ignorant at this point in time in that it accepts the fallacy that the human brain can house only one consciousness. And this has nothing to do with mental illness (schizophrenia). Humankind is foolish to assign this negative concept automatically. He limits his cosmic horizons to a tragic degree!

In perceiving the question and possible answer to #2, we first remind you of the greatest rule: Be of goodness. Be of good intent. Once surrounded with this light, once connected to this God Consciousness - then all contacts and explorations can only broaden the horizon and bring unconditional love!

Many people do not realize that, indeed, contact is being made because they fail to identify the beginnings of contact within their own thoughts. Remember, in contact and subsequent channeling, another mind/soul drifts into your head. It drifts gently, peacefully, and lovingly. It does not take over at will but waits for your "ok." It is sensitive and of goodness. Therefore, you may fail to know it is there!

However, if you are finely tuned and intuitive, you will suddenly suspect that the thought patterns which are coming to you so very beautifully are not quite your familiar thought patterns.

Now, we hasten to explain that you are also capable of beautiful universal thoughts and inspiration. But just as you can discern between Beethoven and another genius like John Lennon, so you can discern the channeled information from your own thought. Remember, another being is linked to you, is sharing consciousness with you. At first it is subtle so as not to scare you or force you into contact (even though you may have requested it).

It is a sign that you are sharing consciousness with a being of goodness in that the initial contact is so gentle, peaceful, and loving as to be hard to differentiate from your own familiar thought process.

Remember, you cannot contact or channel a being who is too radically different in mind/soul wave from your own (this is another reason we say, "Be of goodness."). However, this also makes it hard at first to discern.

Contact is also being sought from higher realms. In other words, they are reaching out to you as you are reaching out to them. You can tell that contact is urgently desired when you have a great and illogical need to explore the unknown, to gain universal knowledge - and also when your life seems suddenly manipulated so as you will indeed have time and opportunity for more meditation, study, and possible contact.

First comes an inkling of contact as you learn to realize that there is a sharing of consciousness at times within your head. The consciousness will be beautiful and loving. Channeling is a gift but also a learned skill. Do not expect to channel at first but only to discern a shared consciousness. However, everyone has the ability to channel! Most people do not become channels just as most people do not become famous pianists; however, everyone can play the piano with a bit of effort.

In perceiving the question and possible answer to #3, please meditate upon the meaning of the word "channel." Water runs in channels and so does a stream of consciousness. Mind/soul waves run in channels (these may also be called frequencies).

The "stuff" which makes Beethoven's music great is *energy*. Energy (the spiritual stream of consciousness) runs in channels - in eddies, ebb tides, swells, and currents. It is much like restless water.

On first contact, the water hardly touches you. It washes into your mind in gentle, tiny, loving streamlets. This is the time to be sure you are of good intent and that the visiting stream of consciousness is therefore of good intent, giving loving, positive input.

If you wish, you may experience this tiny stream of consciousness again during meditation. Once contact is made, it is almost always accessible again. The higher consciousness wants you to try contact again but it is up to you.

Gradually you will begin to tune into the frequency, to allow the stream of consciousness to wash over you whenever you wish. It is a beautiful, unparalleled experience and one which wise, mystical people have spoken of and sought after for ages. It is deeply and profoundly a *cosmic experience* and a time of growth and enlightenment for your mind/soul. It is a time of teaching. It is also wonderful for the higher consciousness' mind/soul because he or she is very happy to be able to make contact, to help, and to inspire.

If you keep at this contact, if you allow the waters to wash over you often, the messages will become more clear, more lucid, and more helpful.

At this point, whether actual channeling occurs depends partially on the compatibility of the human and the other consciousness. Occasionally the two are totally compatible and are in fact soulmates. Other times, the contact with the human has been established since childhood and worked on very actively by other consciousnesses as well, for many years. In these cases, channeling would almost certainly be the result eventually.

Basically one must remember that an open, broad, beautiful channel of flowing water was first started as a tiny streamlette. To channel again and again is to constantly widen the channel. Remember, all things are possible - and all lifeforms have the ability to reach higher levels of being!

In perceiving the question and possible answer to #4, we first must understand that any dimension is made up of seemingly physical features which the mind/soul creates and perceives around itself.

Therefore, if you wish contact with higher realms or if you are diligently working on attempting to develop the ability to channel, you must create a consistent atmosphere for yourself each time to seek contact. This atmosphere must be reflective of the higher dimension - the physical world of that higher dimension - which you wish to contact.

First, have objects which represent to you objects in the higher dimension (or on the other planet if your consciousness prefers this concept). Through out the ages, psychics, mystics, and channels have found that rocks, crystals, sea shells, pine cones -

natural objects - best make the transition from one dimension to another. In other words, if you possess a shiny, lovely multicolored rock which you always rub and hold when you meditate, then this rock will go with you (and manifest!) in the higher dimensional frequency to which you will be going during your meditative session. This special rock will represent your journey, will enhance it, and make it easier each time for you to go. It is highly recommended that you have special rocks, crystals, or other natural objects. It is surprising how much easier these items of meditation make your search for contact. They become objects of both dimensions. They become *teleports*. They are a reality base, a physical perception, in both worlds, for both minds. And they are a safety rope because they will give you a solid physical reality as your mind begins to join the ebb and flow of the cosmic energy. To create an atmosphere of a higher dimension, incense or some mystical, lovely fragrance is urged. Find a fragrance which stimulates your mind/soul and use it every time. If there is particular music which puts you in a distant, mystical mood, play it for your meditation and contact session as well.

Next, find the time of the day or night and the place which best represents an environment in which both consciousnesses will be at ease. The higher realms know and love nature (which is cosmic energy manifested in Earth's atmosphere). Nature is always a good place to be. However, if you are more at ease in the quiet, secure solitude of your own living room in the evening, then make this "headquarters" for both your mind/soul and that of the higher mind/soul - make this their common ground, their intersect point. Candles are very helpful to some people, especially if they have chosen a private, indoor location for their contact sessions.

All in all, remember that you are creating an atmosphere where both you and your higher contact will feel at home. You would not, for instance, find it easy to channel in a room full of Twentieth Century people chattering about the stock market or in the middle of a street filled with Twentieth Century autos!

Once you begin to find the key for allowing the water to wash over you - channels from higher consciousness levels will surely open to you because they wish this contact as much as you do. To be a conduit for The Light is a noble experience!

May the healing light of goodness surround
you, always Tibus

CHANNELING This is Tibus. I come to

you in love and light.

Questions to be asked in this transmission:

1. Does the world in which you live exist in the mind of humankind only? Why is everyone in the world a victim of the money system?

Why is materialism so important in this world? How can materialism be put into perspective and conquered in your personal life?

2. "Humankind may well be but a dream of God's sleeping mind..." What is meant by this concept? Do humans create "dream people" in their sleep?

What part of the world around us is a part of God's Mind? Are we hopelessly surrounded by humankind's creations alone?

3.   "War begins in the minds of human beings. Since this is so, the minds of human beings must also be capable of ending war."

What does this wise statement ultimately tell us about humankind's mind and its connection to God's Mind?

4.   What is God Consciousness? Where is God Consciousness? Can it transcend the daily world?

In perceiving the question and the possible answer to # 1, we must use our gifts of prophecy and rise above the Earth timeline to a period when humankind first emerged on this beautiful blue/green planet.

We can see that, in the beginning, there was no money system, no complex society, no materialism.

Now, of course a race cannot stand still. It is a responsibility before God for a cosmic being to use intelligence, intuition, abilities to evolve. Human kind certainly could not remain in the primitive stage. However, many paths could have been taken by the human race. The path it has chosen to travel is one which is crippled by the "money system," a materialism of staggering proportions.

It is humankind's responsibility to perceive the damage this system causes to so many fellow human beings. It is humanity's obligation to stand back and examine the society he has created and then strive to correct it in places where it is negative and damaging. A few individuals do this; thus you are reading these transmitted words. However, the human race as a whole strives only to reinforce its materialistic ways. One man "lords over" another simply because he has collected more money, often through negative means. And so, often the decent individual becomes more of a victim of the money system than does the more greedy, aggressive individual. The entire system becomes inverted, off-center, and out-of-balance.

Those who are sensitive to cosmic energy are also sensitive to the "bad vibes" of the negative money system with its accompanying materialism. These gentle people (like yourself) become very frustrated and angry over the injustice of it all and don't seem to play the game as well as other people do who do not feel this resentment toward it.

However, those who lose their humanity to the materialistic system are the ones who get hurt the most, though they may have collected a huge mass of the "green stuff." Thus, all are hurt by this dominating, artificial system. Many good luck charms are sold as a "magic" way of overcoming the money system. Sometimes these charms do have power but this is because of the power of your own mind/soul. If you want out of the money system's viciousness badly enough, you can make a charm work. However, the power comes from within you. You *can* overcome, whether you use meditative aids/ tools or whether you do it entirely with the strength of your being.

A first step to escaping from the grasp of materialism and money problems is to do exactly what you are doing: Look at it in perspective! Become fully aware that the system is not God. It is an artificial system which humankind has imposed on itself. This realization in itself breaks a part of the hold the money system has on you!

Everything in the world which is artificial (man-made) exists only in the mind of Man. For instance, if a man thinks up a concept for a shoe store and then *acts* on his mind's thought, he creates a shoe store within his society. The minds of other men perceive this shoe store, make it a thriving business by patronizing it, and it continues to exist in the mundane world.

133

Materialism is important because humankind makes it important. Humanity is a victim of its own artificial system. While no one with a physical body can escape the materialistic system completely unless he or she goes to live on top of Mt. Everest, a person can become less of a slave to money by not allowing money to dominate life. One should resist worrying about it constantly or obsessively. If you do refuse to be its slave, you will find that your mind can begin to overcome the money system. In other words, a first step toward solving money worries is to refuse to participate in the stress and game playing which the materialistic system forces upon one. It takes a bit of mind power, but you *do* have a powerful mind/soul - powerful enough to overcome this man-made "god."

In perceiving the question and possible answer to #2 and #3, we first must realize that the world around us is full of objects and forces which are not creations of humankind's mind but creations of God's Mind.

You have simply to look at nature to realize that God's Mind has created a very mystical and beautiful world all around you.

Look out your window: You see Man's Mind at work - and you see God's Mind at work. These two compose reality.

Now, we know that God's Consciousness is in each and every lifeform as well as being everywhere in the universe. When we look at art or listen to music, we are enjoying a human-made reality but one which is based on the God Consciousness within each man (or woman). This of course is true of many wonderful things in life, right down to a birthday cake which is human- made but which is a universal joy and a way of expressing love - which is

Here is the key: the universal God Consciousness within you is the part which can save you from being a victim of the artificial world around you which seems to worship money and materialism.

If we truly look, if we truly *perceive,* we will know that we are not surrounded by human creations alone. Our world *is* what we perceive it to be. If we feel buried by the materialistic world, then we are buried by it. If we feel we are a part of the universe, if we let our spiritual self run free, then we can rise above the materialistic world. We can put the often ridiculous materialistic world "in its place."

At this point, we will ask: Does God dream? Does the Creator Spirit dream? Does the Life-force create thought-forms just as you do in your dreams - the dreams you have which seem very real? These dreams of yours have details in them; they are colorful, complex, and meaningful.

We may consider the fact that, since all life has a spark of the God Force within, perhaps it is that same spark which is a part of the Creator's dream. It is that spark which is us, which is our eternal spirit. We are detailed, colorful, complex and meaningful and we are of God's Mind (God's Consciousness).

A skeptic might say, "Perhaps God is a dream in the mind of humanity..." To this we say, consider the truth that the two minds/souls (that of God and of Man) are so entwined, so linked - that this statement as well may also be true. How can anyone separate humankind from the universe? How can anyone state that cosmic energy is a one-way street?

What an individual on Earth must do is align himself or herself *more* with the universal energy than with the materialistic world. What the individual on Earth must do is to call on the God Consciousness within himself more than the force of the money system, which should be viewed as a "demon" of sorts.

We do not transmit that you can totally forget about the money system while being evicted from your house! However, if you place the thrust of your being into the God-created part of the world around you, then you stop putting unnecessary energy into the human-made part of Reality.

As a student of metaphysics, you know that the more energy you put into an endeavor, the more active it becomes. There are many misconceptions about metaphysics; one is that the power of the occult mind can cause bad luck or a "hex" to be put on a person. The mundane world seldom realizes the positive side of this axiom: To concentrate one's mind powers on *helping* another person can be most helpful to that person! At any rate, we know that the more mind-energy put into a subject, the more powerful that subject becomes. Now, think of the mind-power you have put into the money system (the money "demon"). People give it more and more power all the time. Refuse to do this, except where absolutely necessary. You will find as time passes that it becomes less of a necessary problem because you are no longer giving it the energy of *worry*. And so, the times when it is absolutely necessary to concentrate on it become less frequent, too.

Yes, you are surrounded by humanity's creations and you are flooded by the worries the money system heaps upon you. However, you are also surrounded by God's creations - the most precious of which is within_yo«. This is where you should put the energy of your mind/soul. It will free you from the other system, the other reality. It can even help those mundane problems ease up and eventually be overcome. Stop giving your mundane problems more strength over you. Often they have you wrapped around their little fingers!

We have transmitted information on the gift of prophecy which is within you. It is this gift more than any other which can help you find the God Consciousness part of your mind/soul, the part which can help you overcome the materialistic system. You must gain perspective! You must gain perspective on who you are as a cosmic citizen. You must gain perspective on your world, where it has been, where it is now, where it is going. Rise above the mundane flow and see the full universal picture.

"War begins in the minds of human beings. Since this is so, the minds of human beings must also be capable of ending war."

We of the higher realms, those slightly above you on the Awareness Mountain, can guide you as we are attempting to now; we will do this as much as we can - as much as humankind will possibly listen to us. However, the key is contained in the above quote. *Your* mind/soul as a being who is in human form at this time - is *the* one who can and must create a brighter Reality.

It is very important to explore the many aspects of yourself which compose the Whole Self. This includes past lives (parallel aspects of your Whole Self), it includes exploring your gifts of precognition, intuition, and prophecy. This includes exploring the other cosmic beings who are there for you at any time, such as guardian angels and star guardians. There is so much involved in the individual being which you can *use*\ These various aspects, experiences, gifts - are all a part of the God Spark within you. Sadly, they often go neglected because the human-made part of your reality dominates.

Never forget that blessed nature is *always* there for you, as a magnificent manifestation of God's mind and soul. You are also a part of that same magnificent nature.

The power of God, the Creator Spirit, is also your power. God Consciousness is inside as well as outside.

May the healing light of goodness surround you, always,
Tibus

14

ALTERNATE DIMENSIONS

TIBUS CHANNELS REGARDING ALTERNATE DIMENSIONS

On one thing scientists and theologians agree: Alternate dimensions do exist!

Star people know this also but for us, it is as if we approach the truth from the inside, going outward. We *know* there are other dimensions not because of scientific theory (though we feel gratified that it supports our feelings), and not even because of a religious belief (though we are equally glad that religion in its pure form fits in beautifully with our knowledge).

Our knowledge of the existence of other dimensions can best be described as homing instinct. We *know* alternate dimensions are "out there" because we somehow belong in one of them. For some crazy reason (at least "crazy" until we figure out our star mission), we are simply in the wrong place!

Ordinary people have great difficulty in understanding this fact. They have no concept of this feeling of displacement - this lifelong feeling of displacement - because they are not displaced! Of course everyone hopes they will "go to heaven," as religions have taught them. However, we star people know that this is much more than reaching for heaven, or hoping to go to a better place upon death of the physical body. This is a solid, constant longing for Home...for a different mind frequency, a different world, a different time.

We know from our knowledge that this dimension for which we yearn is a *higher* dimension in terms of sensitivity, decency and gentleness because so many of the practices in the mundane dimension are cruel, barbaric, and downright incomprehensible to us. This is *the* problem we have had with this place since early childhood! Star people often ask me how they can convince others of this *higher* dimension connection we feel. Many people tell us that *any* connection or feeling of communication with an alien dimension is a negative in itself. If this is so, then the human race is stagnant...and as we know, stagnation is the only true death for the essence (soul). Sadly, it is virtually impossible to have others feel what we feel, know what we know. We can appeal to their intelligence and sensitivity in explaining the Home Dimension's guidance toward peaceful ways, towards unconditional love and joy, but the truth often manifests itself that we *are* alien here and that they simply cannot and will not understand. What we must do above all is to keep in contact with our inner guidance which WE KNOW TO BE OF GOODNESS! We must keep the close contact with SELF who has always vibrated on a more refined and gentle frequency than the world in which it finds itself. Once we do this, more communication with the Home Dimension opens. Trust yourself, Star Child!

While scientists tell us that they are discovering, through quantum physics, that there are an infinite number of intersecting dimensions at any one point in Space/Time and that MIND seems to be the key to traversing these adjacent worlds...and while ministers tell us that there are indeed higher realms which have worked with the human race and which have sent saviors and prophets...while all of this is going on around us, we star people nod knowingly, often with tears in our eyes and sigh, "I know that already! I've always known that. But how do I get home?" For us, a "higher realm" is not an abstract. We look for the home frequency just as someone else might say, "Now where did I park the car?"

"Where did I lose myself from the home dimension? Did I truly volunteer for this lifetime? How big a fool can I be? How do I get back?"

While it is true that we do have missions here and that we did volunteer, it is also our obligation to self to ask these questions and to try to return home. When the time to return home does arrive, and we have not begun these pathways toward the home dimension, we will have difficulty. In other words, when we do find the path home, it will be the time for returning home. We create the path home as much as our co-workers on the home side create the path.

An analogy: If someone is trapped in a cave-in, he or she must scramble toward the rescuers digging away on the other side. He or she must dig the rocks on the inside of the cave-in as the rescuers dig from the outside. It may be that there is only a tiny opening to squeeze through at the proper moment before another cave-in occurs. And so the trapped person *must* be at the opening, not resting on the other side of the cavern! In this same way, we must always remember that this is a *dual mission*. We work from this side to create conduits into the home frequency just as much as our co-workers work at it from their side. We agreed to this *before* the mission began. This is a vital part of the entire mission: To *create* the energy vortex/pathway home. If we do not try, no one on Earth has a chance. On a more selfish basis, we certainly shall never see home again.

We *can* do it. We can do it individually. We can do it collectively. In this way, we can create home itself...for it is otherwise not reachable and therefore might as well be non-existent. When Tibus and others of The Federation tell us that we are *equals,* not inferiors, they mean that we therefore have the responsibility to tunnel out from our earthly existence. Together, we and they *can* work miracles but it takes both sides! We cannot stand by, awaiting doomsday, sitting on the opposite side of the cavern criticizing the mundane world. We must be at the opening/doorway and we must help create that doorway as well!

TRANSMISSION #1

This is Tibus. I come to you in Love and Light.

What is an energy vortex?

Quite simply, it is a place where several kinds (frequencies) of energy come together to form a focal point - an intersection of energies.

What is a dimension?

Quite simply, it is a "place" wherein one frequency is dominant. Within the bounds of a dimension, most minds respond only to this dominant energy.

An energy vortex is therefore as if oil were dropped into a whirlpool of water. You may see a swirl (energy charge) of the non-dominant energy of a given dimension, you may feel a doorway opening into the home frequency from time to time.

This "wash-over" may happen either because you are near a natural energy vortex such as Mother Earth offers in various places at various times, or you may have psychically/ telepathically created this wash-over of dimensional energies through your own meditation and/or mind power.

Here we must clarify what we mean by "power" because this word often has a negative connotation, especially to star people who have seen how power in the earthly sense can corrupt and do harm.

To us in The Federation, power is merely energy, pure in itself. To have life is to have power. This is as it should be. Life takes many forms (and thus we refer to "lifeforms"), but it is *life* itself which chooses to manifest in these various ways. This *life* takes its power from the God Force and - just as you form dreams at night - life forms itself into various manifested realities. Yet there is an infinite variety of *life* forms throughout the universe and in this fact, we rejoice!

On mundane Earth, there is much m*isuse* of power. It is interpreted almost totally in the egocentric, non-spiritual sense of power (political power, military power). Our star people by nature do not misuse this power nearly as much as mundaners do. This is precisely the reason our star people are not big financial successes, in most cases. We need not dwell on power used negatively!

I wish to remind you at this time that we have spoken of frequency wash- overs. You have all experienced this phenomenon when feeling the very simple yet eloquent connection to the Home Side. You have felt a washover of dimensional energies when you feel close to - or feel communication with - the Special One. Also, of course, the viewing of visions, the experiencing of miraculous yet unexplainable feelings, healings, and memories represents a dimensional wash-over. Yes, your Special One and co-workers on the Home Side help...but you have been equally involved in this creation of a vortex (and use of it). Please remember that if your mind and essence (soul) is not participating, Home cannot be interacted with or reached at all!

We have established that you have all experienced wash-overs. These might be called "baby" vortexes for the principle is the same, though the *amount* of power involved is less (than to actually create a working dimensional vortex/door).

Remembering the oil swirl on water and the definition of a vortex, consider that these vortexes can lead to other places. One may follow either the dominant water, or one may follow the oil swirl to its source. If two (or more) frequencies intersect and one is sensitive to the alien frequency, one may follow it. We hasten to

141

add that this is not as easy as it sounds (as sad as this may seem to a Star Person trying to return Home, it is a fortunate thing that dimensional slippage/ "slide zones" is not a common phenomenon in the universe!). We also add that obviously it is much easier to follow the alien frequency intersecting with the dominant frequency *if* Nature's energies are helping you.

In other words, if you create a dimensional door psychically, this is a much more difficult door to go through than one already established in Nature, which can supplement your own psychic energies. Both together are stronger than one, so we of The Federation also turn to natural energy gates (doors) both on Earth and throughout the galaxy for help in dimensional travel.

Another important aspect is that one can only pass through a dimensional door if doorways are open on both sides of the corridor. In other words, visualize an energy vortex as you would visualize a hallway with doors at both ends. If you are standing at one end of a hallway looking through an open door, what will you see? First, you will see the hallway itself - and the door at the opposite end of the corridor.

If the door is closed and there is no way to unlock that door, it would be impossible to proceed down the hall. On the other hand, if you look down the corridor and see that the far door is open, then it is time to pursue your explorations.

And so, the first skill which one must acquire is to know *when* the energies are *right,* not partially right or at half-strength. As you all know, beloved, some days - and particularly some nights - are (simply put) more psychic than others. Sometimes the energies wash in of their own accord, and other times, no matter how hard you try, it just doesn't "get off the ground." Do not feel frustrated by this or feel that you alone in this problem. Other Star People experience it all the time. We experience it as well.

The second important skill to acquire is that of sensing where the energies are washing in from (what frequencies are intersecting with the mundane one). If you are a person of basic goodness, this problem is 99% solved. In other words, the Home Energies zero in on you as well as visa versa. You are spiritually protected. And so, if you are meditating on the Home Dimension and the energies are high, the Home Frequency will be seen, felt, and experienced., .and if there *is* a vortex open on both ends, then the path indeed leads Home.

For example, if you were using psychic energy - as Star people never do - to "get" another person (this being in the stereotyped sense of casting a curse or making bad luck for another person), then obviously as energies open up, you would not find Home but rather a lower dimension. Remember, you are tunneling out from your side as well. You are creating...and so the dimension you reach is what you create. Yes, Home exists on its own..but in searching for it, *you* make your own path. And yes, we help. But if you insist in saying you wish to go to a beautiful mountaintop when in fact you keep walking around in circles in a factory area of a big metropolis, your Special One and other guides cannot, by universal law, *force* you to head for the mountaintop. We can advise, indicate, nudge... To put the concept of this paragraph in a nutshell, *be of goodness!*

Dimensional doorways and vortexes are like roads and streets on planet Earth. There are thousands of them and not all of them will get you where you want to go, either for a meditative experience or an actual trip back Home.

Please interiorize this statement: Your own intuition must lead the way. Trust your instincts! You are a unique and special essence within the universe. You are one of a select group of Light Workers who sacrificed a lot to help planet Earth at this focal point. The Star Person's intuitive gifts are highly developed. Think for a moment: You can tell when an energy "hot spot" is nearby, correct? Even if you do not know how to use it, you can tell when psychic energies are high. Using that same intuition, you must tell the difference between a Homeward bound energy vortex and a negative one - or one which is simply o.k. but does not lead Home (in scientific terms, we mean a parallel dimension to the mundane one which is not of exceptionally high energies). An example of an energy vortex which is not negative but which does not lead to a higher dimension would be that of a cemetery on Halloween. The celebration of Halloween creates strong energies and cemeteries certainly hold psychic energies, anyway, but one would be less likely to have a transcendingly positive experience there than, for instance, at a high energy spot along the seashore at sunrise.

Of course there is also a door which opens into the spirit world and this door is one psychics have used for ages. There is a close, loving connection which The Space Intelligences (Federation) and the Earth Spirit World share, and it is not uncommon or dangerous to feel this connection when seeking the Home Frequency.

For example, Diane was visiting the new home of a friend. This home has much energy...and can indeed be helpful in contacting the Home Frequency. During a psychic/meditative session with her friend, Diane encountered a *small ghost.* The spirit-child could be seen visibly, standing in friendliness and curiosity, attracted by the psychic energies. It was learned that the child, a girl named Millie, had died in a neighboring swimming pool.

This is an example of another dimension being reached while in search of the home frequency. It was not a negative encounter, energy, or dimension. However, it was not the place being sought. Intuition/psychic sense and inner guidance told Diane that this was *not* a dimension to which to make a permanent pathway.

How can you use the power of an energy vortex for seeing into/visiting the Home Dimension and for ultimately finding the permanent pathway/ frequency back?

Remember, the energy which emanates from a *Home vortex* will attract you, because its energy is *your* energy. If raw, natural energies are used (for instance, the psychic feelings one has during a wild storm), remember that you can turn them into the Home Frequency through the very goodness and "star quality" of your personal energy. When you are on the pathway to returning Home, the wonderful feelings are indeed intuitively and soulfully evident. How can you miss them! And before the final pathway is made, you may draw energy from the Home Frequency for survival on earth, so it is a two-way street. You draw strength and power from the Home Energy, thus increasing your energy flow, thus giving you strength to get a few steps closer to Home. You therefore find it easier to move the rocks blocking your pathway out of the cavern from *inside* as well as waiting for co-workers to help from the *outside.*

This is indeed a cycle...a sustaining and beautiful cycle. You can always reach the Home Frequency at least this much! In other words, you may not be able to immediately return Home, you may not be able to feel verbal communication from the Star Guardian - or at least, not all the time - but this wonderful, revitalizing Home frequency is always within reach. It does not require extreme psychic ability or spectacular channeling gifts. It is always *there* to help get you through the day.

Dimensional doorways and their thresholds (energy vortexes) are on Earth and in the cosmos for you to use. They are pure creative, cosmic energies which await only the goodness of your star essence.

TRANSMISSION #2

This is Tibus. I come to you in love and light.

As I have transmitted before, star people have many specific home world sources (frequencies). Some are of pure energy dimensions (what theologians would call the angelic higher realms); other star people are aliens in the popular sense of the word (from other planets circling other stars); and still others are of the future (human time travelers).

We are all members of the Federation (also called Space Intelligences and the Higher Realms).

Do not concern yourself as to your specific origin of consciousness because the answer will manifest itself clearly when the time is right.

These diversities are like tributaries flowing into the main river. The Home Frequency is the main river. The specific tributaries may be embarked upon after the main frequency is tuned into.

In short, we may say that your connection - and that of your Special One - is one which traverses trillions of miles of Space/Time but which may also be reached through dimensional shortcuts (doorways). Analogy: An ant can make his way around a 33 rpm record by going around the edge to the "flip" side. An ant can also get to the other side by going through the hole in the center. The latter would be analogous to a dimensional vortex.

There are times of overlap for dimensional intersect points (which exist throughout the universe in infinite number). There are times of wash-over.

When this happens naturally, there can be numerous UFO sightings, paranormal events and/or psychic feelings in abundance. Become skillful at sensing if a particular day (or night) is a psychically- oriented time. Some days simply *are*, other days simply *are not*. These are the days when mundane energies dominate. Become skillful at sensing if a particular geographical spot is high in psychic energy. Return often to this spot once it is found. Attune your energies to it.

145

There are other dimensions involved in The Federation's work which may be called "interim dimensions." When we on the Home Side live on Earth for a while, we often use these interim dimensions. Often when we appear on Earth, we take refuge in these adjacent dimensions (very similar to the mundane one). For example, when a UFO blinks out, right before the eyes of an Earth military jet, it has "hopped" a dimension...but it has not returned directly to the Home Frequency.

Another example: There are numerous reports of UFO occupants "beaming in" (or out) of visual perception. Often a star person encounters the star guardian on the street or elsewhere in public...only to have him or her vanish before one's eyes.

Hopping back to the Home Frequency in this physical way is rather like hopping a twenty foot pond. It is wiser to use the stepping stones of the interim, friendly dimensions. You will come to know of these interim dimensions as well.

However, you must always have the Home Dimension as the target, the goal. The interim dimensions are ones which you need not worry about and which you may not even realize you are visiting. One need only be of goodness in order to avoid the ones you do not want to visit.

An example of a nearly-identical dimension manifesting: Diane and a friend went in the side door of a restaurant, having left their car in a memorable spot in the parking lot. When they turned to leave the restaurant, the side door was non-existent and their car was in a decidedly different spot in the parking lot. This was a slide zone. We took advantage of the natural high energies of that day to illustrate to these star people what an "adjacent interim dimension" truly is.

All star people experience these, both of their own making, and with the help of the Home Side, in order to prepare them for more drastic dimensional changes.

It has been stated before that Earth energies sometimes converge to form a natural energy vortex. Please be aware that these vortexes often (but not always) can be found in rock formations due to natural electromagnetics.

There is *much* in the field of dimensional physics which will become apparent to Earth science in the future. The Federation has many scientists who study this complicated and illuminating subject. However, there is always a quality to it which defies science. It is the God Force. And so, mastery of dimensional doorways unifies science and spirituality by its very nature.

TRANSMISSION #3

This is Tibus. I come to you in love and light.

All planets have natural dimensional doorways. There are those "stargates" which exist in the void and blackness which is space...and Earth science is presently beginning to suspect these exist through their research into black holes and white holes. And so we see that dimensional doorways are *universal* phenomena. Most of the vortexes fluctuate and change location or close up entirely at times. This is the norm. A few remain as infinite phenomena and are memorials to the pure Creator Force.

Before his death, Einstein worked many years on a unified theory which would combine gravity force with space/time energies. Electromagnetics play an important role in this theory, which the human race will soon unravel, (though slightly different than Einstein envisioned) and use. Once this theory becomes apparent to a race of people on a given planet, dimensional travel is theirs to command. As it is now, there are puzzles (such as the disappearances in Bermuda Triangle) but no comprehension. It might be added here that it is not wise to travel into a strong natural vortex anymore than to walk off a cliff., if one is not intelligently, spiritually, knowingly using this vortex! Do not go blindly into, for instance, the Bermuda Triangle! However, its intersecting frequencies certainly are helpful to *those who know how to use them.*

The most startling quality about the culmination of the work which was begun as the Unified Field Theory is that humankind will find himself "touching the face of God" as he explores this scientific revelation. Science and Spirituality, Logic and Religion will become forever and irrevocably melded together. This is the reason why we try to guide the human race, at this time in particular, toward higher spiritual insights (and this is the specific reason for many missions!). The Change Point (indeed, a dimensional change point) should also be called "The Choice Point" for at that time, the human race must choose a higher spiritual plane - or perish.

The natural dimensional doorways of which we have spoken are more active at some times than at others. Why is this so? Our scientists and spiritualists cannot even tell you exactly. We may say, quite honestly, these fluctuations are God's will.

Usually, dimensional passageways are in harmony. When one is open, most are open. When they are open, the entire earth (and the rest of the galaxy, in all dimensional aspects), is bathed in radiant energy - good, positive energy which emanates from the God Force. An example of this is the Healing days held by many New Age groups which unite those of higher consciousness all around Earth at the same hour.

This energy of which we speak can of course be used for spiritual growth, for more enlightened astral travel, for increased powers of concentration. These primal creative energies are like an underground spring - a spring which brings life to the desert and feeds the immortal soul of life everywhere. This is the Life Force.

To use this energy when it is at its highest, find a place on planet Earth (since your mission is there at this time), which feels positive and powerful to you. Sometimes this can be a private spot in your backyard or you may wish to actively search for one in the forest, near a lake or river, in the desert, or the mountains.

Take a place where *you* can feel the power. Just as some people are more sensitive to temperature changes while others are more sensitive to barometer changes, so some dimensional doorway's energies are more suited to you than others are. In short, find a place *which makes you feel like the Home Dimension will make you feel.*

Once you have found that spot, you may rest assured that you are very close to an energy vortex (trust yourself!) and that your soul is indeed absorbing some of the magnificent energy which gave you Life in the first place!

Because your soul springs from the Home Dimension, it is essential that your soul always stay in contact with it (and the way described above is the simplest and yet most effective). This is one reason why energies vortexes exist...because *you* have never forgotten Home. Just as Earth provides air, light, and water for her children, the Home Dimension provides unique energy and soul nourishment, always. This is why you are "different." You continue to draw strength and power from this energy, just as you replenish it and keep it alive in your heart, despite adversities on mundane Earth. The Home Energy is the type of energy which your body and soul can store just as a battery stores energy for future use.

As you know, dimensional passageways are used by us of The Federation as well as by other beings. There is no reason why

149

these passageways are one way streets only. There is nothing in your human physiological structure which makes you non-qualified as a dimensional traveler. After all, you have traveled from the Home Dimension to Earth already!

We Star Guardians use vortexes for travel constantly. The immortal soul is not damaged by energy corridors but rather, is enhanced by them.

Many vortices appear in places which are not easy for you to reach. I have mentioned before the "stargates" in the blackness of Space/Time. Also, vortexes appear high off the ground (though within Earth's atmosphere). This is why so many planes disappear in the Bermuda Triangle. The scientific proof of this doorway is difficult to find because often the actual vortex is high in the air...and also, it fluctuates in exact location. However, the U.S. government does have proof of this and other dimensional doorways...do *not let them tell you otherwise.*

Often natural vortices appear on top of desert rocks or mountain peaks because of electromagnetics. The ultimate "mountaintop" is The Great Pyramid. Its geometric perfection offers an excellent "door opener" but also nature's rocks and mountains, though not perfectly geometrical, offer the enhanced power key of Mother nature's raw energies. Large trees can also draw this energy and so the magnificent forest offers passageways to the Home Frequency.

With practice, you can draw vortex energies of a place to you and you may begin to do this at will, almost every time you visit the place. The first step is to reach out with your intuitive/psychic abilities to ascertain that a vortex is near. Now, narrow it down to the exact location of that special area which you have chosen (and which has chosen you). This process may take several visits to this spot, at different times of day or night.

If your intuition tells you that the vortex is hovering 1000 feet above the ground, you should - with the power of your mind - use your best energy to draw the vortex closer to you. Think of the energy vortex as being sentient, because in many ways it *is* a sentient entity (though very alien in nature from what Earth thinks of as a conscious energy). A vortex is sensitive to an energy which is similar to itself in some respects and so your "star energy" can draw the vortex closer. Although this is not an accurate concept in many respects, we often think of a vortex as an "energy animal" with which contact can be made and nourished. Many times we have found that vortexes seem to follow certain people throughout their lives, and this is a beautiful blessing as long as the person is of basic goodness. Some star people have weird occurrences all their lives - everything from UFO sightings to actual face-to-face meetings with their Home Guides.

If you wish a vortex to follow you, you must be ready for slide zones and other silly happenings such as Diane and her friend encountered when the side door of the restaurant had simply vanished when they turned to leave, and their car had moved in the parking lot. A sense of humor is helpful as energies careen and manifest in sometimes odd ways. THESE WILL NOT HARM YOU. However, if the unknown frightens you, then you are not ready for interactions of this nature. By your star nature, the unknown is more your friend than is the mundane dimension and 99% of star people know and feel this to be the truth. BE OF GOODNESS. You can only open the doors which you wish to open, for your hand (your mind/soul) is doing the opening!

Visualize yourself lying in nature, in full harmony and balance - you are a part of nature. You are lying near or on the spot which you have felt intuitively/psychically to be your energy vortex. When you are in this spot, you feel almost Home. Now concentrate on drawing a vortex to you (this is an intersection point with the Home Frequency). Remember the visual analogy of the oil and water. Attract the oil as a magnet would, so that it swirls toward you.

During this meditation, forget that *time* exists. Of course you must also forget, for the moment, the humdrum hassles and worries. But far above that, simply forget that there is a date, or a clock. Do not be discouraged if you cannot draw the vortex to you in your first several meditative sessions. Remember, this vortex energy is like a wild animal in some ways. Those in human bodies, even star people, can be so impatient!

At first you may only receive a glimpse of Home. Visions. Insights. Memories. Flashes. Then, contact! All of these *will* happen. The permanent path Home is now at least within sight, feeling, memory, and hope.

This "letting go" in a natural vortex setting promises to be a wonderful and enlightening experience. It also allows the vortex to "know" that you are friendly, that you have a positive mind/soul, that you are a kindred energy, and that may work with you. One must *attempt* contact, must lower walls and blocks, before working with dimensional energies can be accomplished. The psychological survival walls which you have put up in the mundane dimension (and which are necessary there), *must be lowered.* This may take some time but it is necessary before a vortex can be attracted.

We realize what a frustrating experience it is: you have learned survival techniques, qualities which help you survive against the cruelties of the mundane frequency...then you are asked to lower psychological defense mechanisms in order to communicate with the Home Side and in order for you to use dimensional doorways.

TRANSMISSION #4

Time travel is a much simplified concept on mundane Earth. It is possible to travel to Earth's past; it is possible to travel to Earth, 1988, from elsewhere/ elsewhen in time. As metaphysics has taught for ages, and as science is now beginning to realize, there is no "time."

Science tells Earth that time seems to be consecutive moments as opposed to a steady and never -fluctuating stream. These moments may be "hopped" just as one skips stones in a creek.

Alternate timelines play an important part in time/ dimensional travel. An obvious example of an alternate timeline is one in which President Kennedy of the United States was not assassinated. Twenty years later, how much different that country - and the world - would have been! And yet, how very similar as well! In an alternate timeline, Kennedy lives still. In another dimensional plane, the dinosaur flourishes; yet, it flourishes side by side with the alternate "modern" timeline in which Kennedy lives, and so on.

You can begin to grasp the complexity! We are dealing here with past/ future time travel and also *alternate* travel to the past/future. You can visit the past as you remember it...you can be in Dallas on the day Kennedy died. Or you can travel to the past where his motorcade was not mysteriously attacked on that fateful day.

We now give you two documented examples of this for your consideration:

In the 1960s, on Earth, a pilot decided he needed to make an emergency landing at a little-used airfield. One of his engines was

152

running hot. As he approached this airfield, he saw World War II planes in active condition and men scurrying around on the ground dressed in typical WWII vintage attire. According to the pilot's knowledge of this field, it should have been deserted. The pilot established radio contact with the field only to discover that it was indeed 1944! Had he flown through a dimensional door? He did not land because his fear was great. We offer the additional insight that his fear over his hot engine may have dropped his psychological shields sufficiently so as to make his psychic mind responsive to dimensional energies as he flew through them. Keep in mind that "the fear factor" is at times helpful in lowering barriers psychically; thus in childhood on a dark Halloween night, you feel certain you have actually experienced "the beyond." By "fear", we do not mean the horrible kind of fear you feel when you suspect there is an intruder in your home. We mean instead the exciting/adrenalin-pumping feeling of being in the forest at night or seeing a UFO close-up! Incidentally, this World War II airfield case was investigated thoroughly and it was certain that no practical joke had been played upon the pilot, who did make it to another airstrip in his own timeframe safely.

Another example of an alternate timeline:

Two women happily visited an old castle, taking particular note of a small chapel area. They noted that the other visitors were all dressed "in costume," as people had dressed hundreds of years before. The women left the castle, having had an enjoyable tour. When they returned the next day, the tiny chapel was nowhere to be found and other visitors were in modern dress. Upon careful examination of old blueprints, the women found that the chapel *was* to have been built, but never *had* been! These women, who were very psychic and New Age oriented people in the first place, had created a vortex through their fascination with the place, and temporarily stepped through it.

This represents not only time travel but travel to an alternate dimension as well...the *alternate* past. Remember, in the women's mundane dimension, the chapel had never been built. And so, we of The Federation give the human race warnings about the upcoming nuclear and natural disasters...but we also transmit that this holocaust can be prevented. Yes, in some timelines/dimensions, Earth does destroy herself. You may enter into a dimension in which this does not occur...an alternate reality. This is part of the mission of the star person - the Light Worker -

to create these alternate realities. The Home Energies will help you, just as we Star Guides help humanity (and just as *you* help humanity).

All past and future dimensions exist side by side with the one in which you now sit, reading this transmission. The future is a conglomeration of unfulfilled prophecies and fulfilled prophecies - a road map with many variations possible for you. Your mind/soul may embark on any number of different life paths in any number of alternate realities. This is why we encourage you never to sit and wait for "doomsday." Doomsday need not come in your reality.

The future is always in question, is always The Question. And yet, it exists, for I am a part of it. It has an infinite number of alternate paths to be considered. As you know, even small decisions made during the day determine the future in major and minor ways. You are all aware of the reality one creates when one makes the decision to marry one person instead of another.

Consider this: Suppose you were planning a trip to the snow-covered mountains but you were told by a trustworthy psychic that an avalanche would occur while you were there. This affords you the chance to engineer your own reality, because if you are injured or die in the avalanche, the timeline will be without your possibly valuable contributions. The human race will not benefit from your contribution. Just as there are changing alternatives for the individual, so there are changing alternatives for the human race as a whole. In this way, new dimensions are traveled by the second, by the hour.

The question also occurs here: In the avalanche, were you "supposed" to die? Did you somehow cheat Death and destiny? Or, if you did die in the avalanche, did you die "before your time?" Both of these questions are examples of "one dimensional thinking." The human race must broaden its perception, must raise awareness and realize that, (1) there is no death for the soul; (2) life itself is much more flexible than perceived.

The concept of "cheating death" is an absurd one as is "dying before one's time." *Both* realities are valid. *Both* exist. Therefore, we must always go forth with the star mission/purpose (growing and developing spiritually and help ing Earth) because *all* alternatives are reality and are aspects of the Whole.

Here we see that to speak scientifically of dimensional travel and alternatives is also to speak of spirituality and the immortal soul. As we have told you, these two fields are not segregated as humankind has assumed and believed. They are instead inextricably bound; they are one and the same. Remember that a "seer" or prophet can step outside the flow of history, outside the timeline. When this occurs, his or her mind/soul is dimensional traveling. A great prophet exists not only inside the timeline and outside the timeline, but simultaneously on all dimensional levels. Jesus is such a prophet.

Past, present, future - and all alternatives of each - are all tied together in a pattern so complex that only the God-mind (Whole-mind) can begin to comprehend. We of The Federation have more of an overview than those who live on Earth. We can and do hop these dimensions, just as humankind will one day..and just as our Light Workers (star people) have always done, whether in conscious recollection or not.

The past is a dimension easier to perceive. If you are in total harmony with the energy vortex, it is possible to travel back in time. However, that is not where Home lies.

The Eternal Now is, of course, always with you, with your mind/soul. The present, however, in terms of history, is non-existent just as "tick-tock time" is non-existent. There is always the micro-second into the past or the micro second into the future.

What is the future? *You* are the future!

All choices are possible at this micro-second for planet Earth. Your star purpose, as your soul remembers so keenly, is to help the mundane dimension you inhabit during your human lifetime...choose the good path, the peaceful path, the free path, the universal path. And then you will find Home, leading humanity there.

TRANSMISSION #5

The large governments on Earth are working on ways to use dimensional doors, because they have already found the rudimentary scientific secrets of such phenomena.

The tragic thing is, they do not have the spiritual goodness of which we have spoken so often...to be dealing with these phenomena. Great forces are opened up which may be used much as "The Force" in the Earth movie STAR WARS. The Force can be used for *goodness*. The Force can be used for progressing evil.

155

It is a neutral force. It becomes the God-force when it is used for the positive. One manifests the beautiful God-force by practicing good ness and being of goodness. Of course there is God! The point is: Do Earth governments know this?

There are many paranoid and "spooky" stories in the paranormal and UFO research fields about frightening occurrences which star people or UFO contactees experience. The "enemy" in this case is not true aliens from other dimensions or planets but rather the Earth governments who often pose as "paranormal bogeymen" or simply harass those in contact with the beyond in mundane ways. Thus we have the infamous "men in black" accounts prevalent especially in the 1950s.

As a star person, you must keep a low profile where Earth governments are concerned. We are not always able to protect you from government harassment because we cannot interfere directly in this timeline's flow. If lower psychic forces intercede as occasionally happens, we are more within our "rights" to protect you.

More and more, the so-called super-powers of Earth are discovering that the secret to unlocking great energies doesn't lie in the development of nuclear power or orbiting laser satellites. Instead, they are finding that the secret to great power lies in the minds of individuals like yourself who are keyed into other frequencies. Psychic ability coupled with new technology will give these super-powers awesome capabilities which we can only hope that we of The Federation will not have to *overtly* stop. It is our dearest law that we *not* interfere with the natural evolutionary path of a planet. However, if our worlds as well are threatened...if it threatens the future and also the future of other worlds...we will physically stand at our star people's sides to help avoid catastrophe.

Keep your secrets close to your heart, star person. Again, trust your instincts. Do not feel you must broadcast to the world because yours is a much deeper and more subtle mission than shallow "missionary" work. Your task is literally to change the frequency of a dimension!

TRANSMISSION #6

We have attempted to guide you clearly and specifically as to how to use a natural vortex which you can find, if you only look. Remember, choose the natural energy flow which feels friendliest to you...and be patient as your two sentient energies merge. Remember also that there are some points in time (a particular day or night or part of a particular day or night), which has higher psychic energies for you personally than usual. And so, you must *feel* the time and place within yourself (by "psychic", we refer to all which has been spoken of in these transmissions).

On occasion, one can create a dimensional door within his or her own home or property. These are temporary doors, forced open through sheer power of mind, plus natural energies of the day or night.

Star child, as you begin the creation of the intersect point which will lead you to the Home Frequency, cleanse yourself in the light of God and goodness as you meditate. Do so on a night (or day) when you feel totally close to Home (do not attempt this when you are angry, hurt, frustrated, or low on energy).

After the cleansing, visualize yourself on a stellar path, strewn with sparkling stars. You may walk along this path and the stars will be as flowers all around you...glistening diamonds in the blackness of space.

You begin to relax, your breathing becomes slower. All the cares of the days are forgotten. Your mind/soul are floating, totally at peace, completely safe and secure.

Ahead on the shimmering star path, you perceive that there are ten stars. You begin your journey at the tenth star which is an electric white/blue color, the size of a large sunflower at the side of your path. You can feel the beauty and the consciousness within this star.

Now continue on to the ninth star. It is delicate and tiny, much like a violet. It is deep purple. You know it well and love it dearly. You feel a release of tension, a release from worldly cares...and the Home Energy encompasses you.

The eighth star is emerald green. It is as a wild flower in a fragrant forest. It is a healing star, a Home star. Allow it to help you, healing the hurts and injuries which the human lifetime has brought you.

The seventh star is yellow and you know this one as Sol, home star of planet Earth. Sol is highly sentient in itself, giving warmth and light to all who seek. Let go of the frustrations you have felt while under Sol's light on planet Earth. All is forgiven. Remember that Jesus also forgave his earthly brethren.

The sixth star is rose pink/white. This is the star of joy, the unconditional love one feels while traveling the path Home. Revel in its beauty now.

The fourth star is the color of warm orange. It is the star of friendship. Remember friends and companions, your comrades on Earth who are also Light Workers. There are also those beings whom you cannot see with human eyes but whose presence you have always felt. They are your spiritual family and your own Special One (star guardian). Let the love flow!

Walk on along the star path. The third star is pure, sparkling red. This is the color of life, of energy, of passionate love on an unconditional basis. Feel re-energized as you pass it because the love you have sent out is returning to give you new life.

The second star is gold. It is intense and magnificent. It is the *Question* and

Answer rolled into one celestial flower.

The first star on this path is of purest energy, glowing with all the colors combined in swirling patterns. It is the God-force and in order to comprehend it consciously, we see all the colors turning into a massive white glow as they swirl. This is an energy intersect point where the love of *all* dimensions, all worlds, all galaxies, all times...converge. Your mind/soul communicate with this love and power and become *one* with it. You should work with this star path as often as you wish, in meditation and contact sessions when you wish to reach the Home Frequency, Even though you will not transcend Home to stay at this moment, you will know the path well in your mind/soul when the time comes that *you must* find the way Home.

If you wish a more physical energy vortex to be created, you may use this star path we have given you as a *beginning.*

After you have reached *the* place at the end of the path, remain in this deep state of concentration. Now, through creative visualization, *create* a doorway/ vortex in your backyard (or wherever there is privacy). Or, you may even enhance the energies of the natural special place away from your house by solidifying it as a solid, positive vortex in meditative visualization, then physically travel to that special place once again.

Whether you are concentrating on your own property or that special place some distance away, tell yourself as you do meditative creative visualization that you are now projecting each step of the way to this vortex so as when you get to it, it will indeed be the actual solid vortex you have felt it to be potentially. In other words, when you are through meditating, you visualize how the sun will feel on your face as you physically head for the special place (or if you prefer to do this at night, you will project how the cool night air will feel on your face and how the stars will be out. Look up at the stars and know that they are as real as the star path you are creating for yourself, and visa versa).

Again, we urge you to try this creative visualization when the time is *right* for you and when energies are positive and high.

All that you have ever read, studied, known, felt about Mind over Matter, about metaphysics, about your own "star" nature, about being different in a mundane world, about feeling in contact with higher intelligence, about your belief in God....all is in play now! You *know* the vortex will be in the particular spot in which you have placed it.

The yard is dark and so you gaze toward the far corner to catch a glimpse of the light...There it is, the door!

Star person, in this way, you *can* - temporarily - create a passageway Home to be used for communication, experiencing, healing.

When the time is right, the passageway will be open for you. The time is sooner than you might dream. You must at least know this path well. You know not to be impatient in finding it. One does not run a race in world record time on his or her first race. Remember that all must be in harmony and that time must be cosmically right...your mind/soul must be at full force as must be the natural energies at that intersect point in Space/Time.

Remember also that you are not alone. Remember the analogy to the trapped individual within the cave. There are those rescue workers who help from beyond, as well. But there must be an effort on your part or the path will remain a secret to you.

This is Tibus. I come to you once again in love and light.

This and other transmissions about dimensions are a part of the "digging out" which we on the Homeside are doing as you struggle your way out from your dimension. This is not the only help which you are receiving. We are helping each and every Light Worker in ways which may not be readily evident. And our contact grows stronger and more active each day.

We have told you that the path Homeward blends science and spirituality. It is The Whole. It is the River.

Einstein, the scientist who moved Earth along on her destiny's path, was also a mystic. The Earth scientific community took his theories in their typical absolutist manner and created a set order and dogma out of them. Einstein offered them only as stepping stones along the path. He felt, at this point in time, that nothing could travel faster than the speed of light. His belief was essentially correct but it is also irrelevant (something he later realized but the scientists who started preaching his works as dogma had already closed their minds, until recently).

I will explain why I have called Einstein's work irrelevant: Humankind will not travel faster than light but will instead travel *through* light (as we of The Federation do now).

All matter is composed of molecules (subatomic particles) moving at different speeds. There is always space between these molecules. If you know beyond a shadow of a doubt, that you can get up and walk *through* the wall, you can do so! However, your mind/soul is conditioned to have at least a shred of doubt because it has had to survive in the mundane world. This is not your fault!

Hyperlight speed gives our star ships the ability to move between molecules, between light and time itself. Again, I remind you, you may float down the river on a boat, participating in its movement or you may hop the stones of the river, moving not against it but rather bouncing over its space, not subject to the laws of its motion, momentum, or flow.

If you travel *through* the sub-atomic particles which make up light itself (remember the space between these particles which is already an established scientific fact), then you are traveling faster than a beam of light through which those particles pass. Consider spatial displacement: When you travel through water, the water's molecules are parted and you pass through.

Do not be afraid to consider these "future science" concepts. Do not feel that "perhaps your brain can't comprehend."

It can, it will, it must...for you will be traveling through light in the future, within the lifetime you now live! Mysticism, psychic pursuits (when of goodness), spirituality, meditation... all of these are shortcuts to the science of which I now speak. The mind/ soul need not fully understand every equation or every theory in order to *be,* and to *do!* It is well and good to understand scientifically what is happening and someday soon, the human race will begin to do this. It will begin to do this, thanks to our Light Workers' (star people's) completed mission.

Never make the mistake of excluding science for spirituality, or visa versa. Go with the path which is right for you but never be intolerant of those who stress the other end of the spectrum. In other words, some people are UFO, parapsychology, "Let's-build-a-starship" oriented (science oriented). Other people are purists in the religious, spiritual sense and easily make the connection from the Space Intelligences to the Higher Realms to Jesus. All is in balance! Each person's focal point of concentration is a natural "star" quality of his or her mission and *must* be allowed to flower as it wishes.

Power outages have been and will continue to be a major source of "inspiration" for more scientifically oriented people. This is, of course, not our only reason for causing them occasionally. At this point, be aware that electricity offers a primitive though intense source of energy which is abundant on planet Earth. It is easily located and already harnessed in millions of miles of power lines and cables, focused in transformer stations. Just as you can use a train, car, plane, bike, roller skates, your feet, etc., to go fifty miles, so various concentrations and types of energies can be used in our operations and missions. Power outages cause distractions so that other energy sources can be drawn from, in some crisis instances. Many of you have felt communication from us through electrical energy in your homes (hums, beeps, pulses, etc.). These are forerunners and beginnings to more specific communication.

When the Change Point comes, power outages will be "mandatory" due to all forms of energies being in flux.

Star person, you must know the path Home or you will be lost when the time comes that it must be taken. Know that the alternative timelines and adjacent dimensions must be areas of knowledge and familiarity, not of fear of the unknown.

Whether being re-energized in the Home Frequency or traveling the final star path homeward, you will take to dimensional traveling as the fish takes to water or the bird takes to the air.

Do not let the human fear of the unknown nor all the bogeymen of past religions frighten you. God is everywhere in the universe, not on planet Earth alone. As a matter of fact, your mission is to bring the God-force into more active play on Earth, because God's love is stronger on other worlds! You know this through the Home Energies you so familiar to you. They are more peaceful, more sensitive, more God-like. And so, forget science fiction movies on dimensional travel which ended with the hapless humans meeting ridiculous monsters or "aliens." You know what is in your heart. The God of the Solar System, the God of the galaxy, the God of the universe...responds to *love.* The God-force sends you a constant and never-ending radiant love/ energy. You have only to respond, to be *of* this love, to be in constant contact with it. It protects you in dimensional travel when you are in the unknown. You have only to love God back through loving *all life* - then the bogeymen will disappear from your reality. Fear feeds on itself. Do not let it in.

Dimensional travel is not new to you. You have done it to be where you are right now. You have had command of it and you will again. I promise you that you will walk through the passageway and that Home does await!

We try in many ways to prepare you. You must dig your own path out of the cavern as we work from outside. Do not despair. You are making progress. We share your impatience but that doesn't help much, in moments of frustration.

Please internalize the blending of spirituality and scientific theory. When considering dimensions, no comprehension can be attained without this blending. All consciousness works on energy frequency (mind waves) throughout the universe. The physical body may " go along" if the mind/soul is strong enough to take it along and if the mind/soul wants to be "burdened" with the physical body. Some people hope that this physical burden will be lifted before they transcend, others wish desperately that the physical body go along at the Change Point. This is the concept of being able to pilot a starship and to actually be a starship crew member. Either alternative is possible at the Change Point. That decision is between you and God.

Love transcends time/dimension, it transcends space, it transcends alL.and at this time, I give you my unconditional love, my friends.

May the healing light of God and goodness surround you, always,
Tibus

15

PERSONAL CHANNELINGS FROM TIBUS

FOR ALL STAR PEOPLE

The following section is a compilation of excerpts from personal readings and channelings Tibus and I have done for individual star people. Though these words were intended for individuals at the time they were channeled and written down, it is our belief that all star people can benefit from these teachings.

Each individual channeling is preceded by a "title" which gives a vague idea of what the channeling was about, as well as a date when the channeling was originally done. Sometimes, at the end of Tibus' channeling, I will include my own comments and observations in the hopes of clarification and continuity.

It is our sincere hope that these words will enrich your spiritual development, enlighten your star spirit, and help to guide you along your continuing star path.

DIANE M. TESSMAN,
DD, DL STARLIGHT
MYSTIC CENTER
TIBUS CHANNELS REGARDING STAR GUARDIANS
TAKEN CAPTIVE BY GOVERNMENT FORCES

September 1986

As Diane and I have often mentioned, star people such as yourself do have unique and very specialized spiritual gifts, and it is these gifts and how to use them that I would like to discuss with you during this reading. As you know, many of our star brothers who have visited your planet have been taken captive by governmental forces around your world. Many times, these star brothers manage to "escape" on their own; other times, we are able to "rescue" them using technology which governments of your Earth does not yet understand and for which they cannot defend against. And yet, there are occasional times when our star brothers *cannot* be freed — and as we have often mentioned, the "fate" of these brothers is sometimes cruel.

Those who cannot be freed, and who are to be "permanently

held" by governmental forces, are often placed into cryonic suspension — a means whereby all physical lifeforces of the body can be "suspended," rendering the "patient" completely helpless and at the mercy of the captors. The other thing about this type of "suspension" is that is *does* permit the mind-energy (or astral body) to "travel." In other words, those who are placed into suspension are physically unable to move, and all life functions (such as heartbeat, respiration, digestion, etc.,) are "suspended." On the other hand, the mental/spiritual activity of the mind/brain *cannot* be suspended — and many of our star brothers *do* manage to find a "freedom" of sorts in the astral realm.

There are, of course, many star people who feel this is the "destiny" of those star brothers. And yet, I transmit to you at this time that "destiny" is often a matter of choosing and not a matter of predestined "fate." In other words, we can and should *choose* our own destiny, we can and should *engineer* our own destiny in the best interest of all concerned. We star guides are concerned and saddened over the fact that this *choice* — the fundamental and irreversable choice to *life*— has been taken away from those who have been captured and placed into cryonic suspension.

We remind you again that the mind/soul/spirit is still active and very much alive when the body is suspended -- and therefore, cryonic suspension can and does become a prison which binds the body to "life," and condemns the mind/soul/spirit to a possible eternity in prison.

As an analogy, consider your own nightly dreams. While you sleep, your mind/soul is very much active — dreaming, often travelling on the astral plane. Your body, on the other hand, is inactive and, for that particular time, "useless." In short, even though the mind/spirit/soul is certainly more important, it is fundamentally wrong to deny to any living creature the right to live as a whole being. In short, during your nightly sleep, you have *chosen* to rest; but during the long, cold sleep of cryonic suspension, that choice has been removed and replaced with an order given by some politician a thousand or more miles removed from the reality of the situation.

The "good" thing is that the mind is still active — and can therefore travel the astral plane and still remain in contact with those of us still on board the starships. But the lifeforce itself has been taken away - and it is *that* injustice which we protest and which we encourage *you* to protest as well.

In almost any state in America, there are "top secret" government installations — places which specialize in either weaponry, weapons research, military secrets, and so on. As a star person, you are undoubtedly "sensitive" to the energy of such places. When you travel by one of these installations, perhaps you feel chilled or otherwise "uncomfortable" with the general vibrations of the area. This is very common in installations which "house" those of our star brothers who have been taken captive and who are being held against their will. The reason you may feel "chilled" or uncomfortable is that you are sensing the psychokinetic energy which is expended from a mind trapped in suspension. In a very small way, when you are near to a place such as this, you are sharing a temporary "consciousness" with the being or beings who are inside, who are being held in suspension, and who are essentially reaching out to *you* for psychic help.

Of course, the most important thing is your own awareness of *what* you are feeling as well as what you can do about it. Primarily, we star guides urge you to always test your own spiritual sensitivity — particularly if you live near one of these installations or military bases. Believe it or not, the places which "house" captured extraterrestrials are more prevalent than you might imagine. Which is one reason the national "interest" in UFOs and other such phenomena has dropped and the governmental attitude has become one of denial. In short, *many* different races have visited your world - some more technologically advanced than the Ashtar Command, others less advanced. But among all of those who have visited your world, the government has always had a policy of keeping the information *away* from the public and thereby holding complete control over the eventual "fate" of any extraterrestrial beings who may have been taken captive and/or placed into suspension.

As to what you as a star person can do about it... there are many things. First of all, as we have already mentioned, sharpen your own personal awareness. The first step toward solving any problem is the awareness that it does exist. Secondly, if you live near an installation which you suspect may be involved in housing extraterrestrials, or if you have suspicions about any area, we urge you to probe that area with your mind - with your astral/ spiritual energy. If you still feel that you are on the right track, we then urge you to call out with your mind to those of our star brothers who may be being held physically captive.

Keep in mind that the thoughts/spiritual energy/mind energy of those star guides is still active - every bit as active as yours or mine, and that telepathic communication with these star guides will give you additional information in many areas. Additionally, by attempting to communicate with our captured brothers, you will, in your own way, be alleviating a small part of the terrible *aloneness* which comes with being placed into "sleep suspension" against one's will. Keep in mind that these captured star guides have been taken from *their* loved ones, too. And imagine how you would feel if you were suddenly placed into a unit where you lived forever in a land of endless dreams.

While some dreams can certainly be pleasant, others can be an eternal nightmare if the dreamer is never permitted to awaken. We hesitate to divulge this information for a variety of reasons - not the least of which is that there *can* be a danger to *you* if you are not careful and if you do not continue to employ your precious spiritual gifts. In short, so long as you protect yourself with the White Light of Truth, and so long as you call on your guardian angels and your own Special One for guidance and protection, you will be safe. But please remember, my friend, thatyowr safety must always come first. Wevalue you immensely, and will always protect you and those you love.

Remember also that your thought energies *can* reach those of us who have been unfairly imprisoned on the astral/dream plane - and that by reaching them, we are taking the first step toward freeing them. During the End Times and the Change Point, your course in this direction will become clearer, and we urge you to meditate further on this entire area of thought. In short, open your mind during meditation to the concept of eternal dreams — dreams which you might not choose to dream if you had the choice. That is the "fate" of the star guides who have been captured, and we ask your help in reaching them.

We ask *your* help in reaching these temporarily "lost" companions. Without your unique energies, without your love, your world would be in far worse condition than it is. *You* are the guiding light of the future - for your world, and for those of our star friends who have had the right of choice taken from them.

May the healing light of God and goodness surround you always,

Tibus.

Comment: Finally, I would just like to add that star people must always remember that our star guides such as Tibus, Micha, Ashtar and others are not "invincible." In other words, we are *brothers* and *sisters* — which means, in very simplified terms, that we are "of the same flesh." We have all come to this Earth for a very important mission — and only when we can work together for the betterment of Humankind will that mission be fulfilled.

Also, please keep in mind that our simple *awareness* of this type of thing is vitally important. So long as we remember that we are not alone, we have taken the first step toward the stars... and home. Primarily, it is my impression that Tibus wants us to remember our imprisoned star brothers — and by remembering them, we are increasing our own commitment to help them... just as they have helped us so often in the past, and as they continue to help us as we journey into the future.

Peace, love and light always,

D.M.T.

TIBUS CHANNELS REGARDING WORLD GOVERNMENT, CENSORSHIP & RELIGIOUS FALLACY

October 1986

In this channeling, I would like to discuss with you some of the conditions your world currently faces and what you as a star person can do to change world attitudes and trends which may not be to your liking.

Essentially, as you have undoubtedly noticed, your world is in the grips of many divergent forces at this moment. There is tension due to the expulsion of diplomats from the US, the Soviet Union, Britain, Syria and so on — and as know, these political maneuvers are often the first signs of conflict. In the past, this potential conflict, while certainly a danger to life, was not a world wide threat. Now, however, with the continuing threat of nuclear exchange, any conflict has the potential to become the final conflict.

In addition to the nuclear threat, there is also a domestic threat which is, in many ways, equally as frightening. As you may have heard, there have been recent rulings in certain states which prohibit the teaching of certain books -- among them THE WIZARD OF OZ and THE DIARY OF ANNE FRANK. These books have been deemed by a so-called "supreme court" to be "offensive to the religious beliefs" of certain individuals. Why? THE WIZARD OF OZ was so-banned because it allegedly portrayed witches as being good. And THE DIARY OF ANNE FRANK was banned because "it tolerates all religions."

Essentially, these two books — and others are certain to follow - are being made unavailable to children in certain states because a few so-called "religious" individuals cannot tolerate the concepts which differ from their own. We starguides certainly have no "say" in the matter, yet it has been our experience that censorship in the name of religion can and will lead to the eventual censorship such as exists in many foreign governments. In essence, any religion which states that all other religions are not to be tolerated should be seriously examined — not only by the individuals who subscribe to that religion, but by the law-giving bodies of your government as well. While we realize how radical this may sound to some, we urge you to consider the matter for yourself. We believe you will agree that more wars have been fought in the name of religion, more lives have been taken in the name of religion, more "hatred" has arisen in the name of religion... than in the name of any other collective concept.

In short, when Man begins to use his "religion" as a tool for war, as a tool for suppressing the beliefs of others, then is that religion truly in the name of God or any Supreme Being? The Biblical God teaches us to "love our fellow man," and states that judgement is reserved for Him alone. And yet, with the censorship of books in Tennessee, it is wholly apparent to us star guides that *Man* is taking judgement unto himself.

Other allegedly "offensive" concepts which were mentioed in the trial were as follows:

It was found offensive to certain religions to tolerate the idea of a "world government." (In essence, this means that some religions perpetrate the concept of nations such as the US, the Soviet Union, China, South Africa, and so on. And while each of those nations certainly has a right to exist as an entity unto itself, these "religions" seem to be perpetrating the idea that they *must* continue to exist as entities unto themselves).

In explaining further, allow me to say this: It is *only* when your world becomes united that universal and *spiritual* unity will become possible. In other words, so long as nations exist and co-exist peacefully, there is no problem. However, when those same nations *demand* the right to exist separately and without cooperation with others, your world is doomed to eventual war, your people doomed to eventual annihilation from the face of the Earth — which is where the Biblical God again comes into the picture.

In essence, it is Man's wrongful interpretation of "religion" which has led to your current world condition — at least in certain areas and under certain circumstances. When Man begins seeing himself *as* God, and when Man begins interpreting the Bible or any other religious document wrongfully, Man then dooms himself as a species and as a planet. In other words, if one went back to the original Hebrew transcripts of the Holy Bible, Man would discover that at no point does that Word state there is only *one* religion, nor would he find anything denouncing a "world government." In short, *Man* has placed his imperfect values on the "perfect" word of God — whether that "perfect word of God" is found in the Bible, in the Koran, in the Dead Sea Scrolls or in Nature itself. And as man is, by nature, an *im*perfect creature, it is inevitable that Man's values will fail him and lead to destruction of all he knows.

As an analogy, the term "human error" has become quite common in this day and age - and with good reason. Humans *do* make errors. Nature and/or God do not. By nature, your species is non-violent — by *nature,* not by training or social customs. In other words, by *nature,* all living things retract from violence or the threat of harm. By *nature,* man fears death — not only the death of himself, but the death/extinction of his own species.

Therefore, it is possible to assume that only your social and political structures have made it "acceptable" to fight wars in an attempt to superimpose one set of beliefs over another — i.e., a war fought to make the world Catholic, for example, instead of Baptist, Methodist, Buddhist, and so on. By *nature,* man is basically an inoffensive, tolerant creature — sharing his planet with a variety of other lifeforms. But when social and political values intervene, that *nature* can be upset and even destroyed, leaving Man vulnerable to himself and those around him.

As a star person, we strongly urge you to consider these concepts at length, meditating on the concept of human *nature* and human *error.* In short, we ask that you look into yourself to determine where your personal beliefs lie in this area. Perhaps you have never considered that a "world government" would be offensive. It *shouldn't* be offensive — for it certainly represents a possibility for world peace, an end to wars, and an opportunity for all the peoples of your planet to co-exist in harmony. But remember that there *are* those who *do* find the possibility of a world government to be a terrible threat — perhaps because those individuals are simply frightened that it wouldn't be "their" government, perhaps because they have become so inundated with propaganda that they are afraid even to give it consideration.

When we speak of "world government," we must understand that we are speaking of *unity* and *peace* — neither of which has existed on your planet in its history. In short, a world government would *have* to be a mutually beneficial one — for Man's nature is *also* not to live in captivity, not to live in an oppressed state, not to be a slave or pawn of *any* government. And when we consider this, it becomes obvious that Man's very nature would not allow a *bad* world government to exist. Man's rebellious nature would be awakened, and any world government which was *not* mutually beneficial would certainly fall and be replaced by another... and so on... until eventual world peace became a reality.

As with anything, it is not destined to be "easy," but it is destined to be. And when such concepts are "fought" against in the name of religion, we urge the star person such as yourself to look more closely at that religion, in order to make the determination as to whether it really is a religion, or whether it is Man's wrongful interpretation of the world and even of the Word of God and/or Nature.

Additionally, on the topic of censoring books and dictating what can and cannot be taught, we ask you to consider that *awareness* is the key to continued existence for your world and her people. In short, if everything that someone found offensive was censored, your world would exist in total darkness, and awareness would become impossible. In other words, it is only through *knowledge* of other ideas and other ways different from one's own that one can grow and learn to make intelligent choices for himself. By censoring, Man only makes certain knowledge more desirable — and, like Adam and the apple, Man will inevitably misuse forbidden knowledge. Whereas, if that knowledge had never been forbidden in the first place, perhaps the temptation would never have existed to bite into the apple. And yet, if Man tries to *remove* the apple, if he tries to censor ideas and concepts, he is essentially shoving the apple into his own mouth and virtually tasting his own destruction. Again, awareness is vital to the survival of your world — and when even one small book or concept is removed from availability, awareness becomes limited.

Again, we ask you to dwell on these concepts at length - on the idea of "religions vs. God/Nature." God is not a religion, neither is he a Baptist, a Catholic, a Buddhist or a Methodist. The Supreme God/Nature is *all* things, and therefore should represent a tolerance for all things by all people.

As you meditate further on this, I am confident you will discover your own Truth, and that you will utilize that truth to bring awareness to others. Let your Truth be a light which illuminates the darkness — and I know you will find others coming to you, asking you where this inner peace comes from. And when you tell them, when you share your awareness, you will be doing one small part of your Earthly mission — bringing awareness and light into the darkness often inhabited by those of the mundane/Earthly vibration.

May the healing light of God and goodness surround you always, Tibus.

Comment: Finally, I would just like to say that the topics of "censorship"
and "world governments" are very close to both Tibus and myself - and with very good reason. There are those who feel the work we do here at the Starlight Mystic Center is wrong - because it does not teach one *specific* religion. For that reason, we have often received threatening letters, our mail has been "audited" on occasion, and our hearts have sometimes been close to breaking because of the intolerance and hatred in the hearts of our fellow men.

I feel very strongly that our world is on the very brink of disaster, and only through continuing to spread awareness and Light will we as star people be able to make a difference in our planet and its attitudes and, especially, its *future.*
D.M.T.

TIBUS CHANNELS REGARDING "THE HOLIDAY SEASON" AND HOW OUR SPIRITUALITY CAN SEE US THROUGH LONELINESS AND PERSONAL PROBLEMS IN OUR DAILY

LIVES

The star person such as yourself is always sensitive to changes — changes in the environment, changes within oneself, changes in the attitudes of others. And it is that kind of sensitivity which can so easily be disturbed at this time of year. As you know, the Holiday Season should be a joyous time — a time for sharing with friends and loved ones, and a time for deep personal reflections. And yet, as our world grows more crowded and the mundane society grows more aggressive, it is important to remember to take care of yourself just as much as you take care of those around you.

As we move into the end of this year, I ask you to take a few minutes each day to reflect on your accomplishments, your spiritual growth, and your goals for your own personal future. For without you, this planet would be a different place. You *do* make a difference, my star friend, and we encourage you to remember that, and to take those few minutes to strengthen your spiritual shields and to meditate on what you would like to accomplish in years ahead.

It is at this special time of year that we star guides again wish to thank you for your spiritual involvement with your planet, with us, and with your own Special Ones. Sometimes, we all tend to take for granted the fact that we *are* special — and star people are among the most unique and special of all beings. Why? Perhaps because you represent to us the future itself, Earth's survival, and the coming of the New Age of Man. Without you, my star friend, the world *would* be a much more empty and lonely place. And though we may not mention it often, we wanted you to know that your efforts are felt and appreciated, and that your presence is experienced among us... just as we hope our presence is experienced within you.

As Diane mentioned, your planet is entering a time of year when there will be much happiness, much rejoicing, much celebration. And yet, there will also be increased chaos — and, in some cases, increased loneliness and despair.

As you know from your own star experiences, the star path *can* be a lonely one — especially before one realizes that it *is* a star path. To explain, remember back to the time before you became aware of your star nature and your star destiny. As a child, you were undoubtedly "different," often set apart from friends and even family — mentally even if not physically. You did not

173

understand why you didn't "fit in"; and for that reason, you were often lonely and perhaps even unhappy at times. You felt that you were not understood by your peers and your relatives, that you were never quite a "part" of what was transpiring around you. And yet, once you discovered your star nature, you could at least understand where these feelings of alienation originated. You could logically comprehend that you *were* different — and that that difference was a source of joy and accomplishment rather than some incomprehensible "negative personality trait" as you may once have believed.

So, in many ways, the key to spiritual happiness and fulfillment is personal spiritual awareness. And yet, now that you have achieved that awareness of who and what you are, you have taken on a great responsibility — the responsibility of helping to "awaken" other star souls who are experiencing those same dark, despairing years that you once travelled earlier along your path.

During this Holiday Season, the spiritual energies of the world will be high. Some good. Some bad. The good energies are for obvious reasons -- sharing, seeing loved ones after long periods of being separated, and so on. But the "bad" energies are often less easy to define -- for they are the energies of those despairing and lonely, the energies of the homeless, the energies of those who do not have the good fortune that the majority of us in the Star Network have achieved.

And so, during this time of year, we ask you to spiritually reach out to these people — not as a "mass consciousness," but as single, individual human beings in need of spiritual guidance and assistance. And we are confident that, by doing so, you will increase your own spiritual gifts ten-fold, as well as helping someone else on toward their eventual spiritual destiny.

In essence, what we are asking you to do is to select *one* person. To do this, I would like to ask you to meditate. Choose a time over the next 3 days that is a time when you will be able to spend at least a hour undisturbed. Establish your "personal solitude frequency" with music, candle light (a yellow or golden candle is excellent for this meditation); and then allow your mind to settle into its contemplative and spiritual meditative state.

Once you have achieved that state, open your mind and heart to the name of one person on the face of this Earth. The first name which comes to you is usually the name of someone who is reaching out. But, more than that, it is the name of someone who is on your own personal energy frequency — allowing the two of you to communicate in this manner more easily. It is also the name of someone who has been reaching out to you — whether they are aware of it on a conscious level or not.

After you have received the name of your spiritual brother or sister, we ask you to send a loving light to that person — the spiritual light of Truth. Remember again that *you* have already achieved your own awareness of your :ar nature and your personal destiny. But the person to whom you are communicating in your meditative state does not yet share that same peace **f** mind and comfort of spirit. Again, it is your responsibility to guide others toward their destiny — and very often this can be done through meditation and a deep spiritual commitment. As your meditation continues, impart to your spiritual brother or sister that they are *not* alone. Encourage them to look into themselves for the answers they are seeking. And, even more, encourage them to open themselves to awareness of their own star nature. Through your spiritual, meditative bond, wrap this other lonely star person in light and love — showing them that there is a place for them, a place in *your* heart and in the hearts and minds of all star people everywhere.

And, most of all, ask them to communicate with you again whenever they feel the need. Encourage your newfound brother or sister to call on you for guidance and support - and be willing always to share the benefit of your own personal awareness with your new charge.

I think you will find that, in the course of a single meditation, you will develop a deep, lasting bond with another living being — a person somewhere who is feeling those same lonely and despairing feelings that you once experienced. And, more than that, try to remember a time when you suddenly *felt* and *knew* that someone was reaching out to you. You may never have seen or "met" this person in the physical world, yet at some point in your life, you began to "know" the truth - and in knowing, you gained the ability to seek awareness and a higher knowledge. Now, when you think about it, the positions have become "reversed." Now, you are the one reaching out to another lonely, aching star soul. You are in the role of teacher and friend. And you have made a spiritual friend who will be with you always — a brother or sister in your star mission, a supportive influence in your daily life.

As you end your meditation, be sure to impart your own inner peace and awareness to your new friend. Assure them again and frequently, that they aren't alone, that there are others like themselves who are on your planet for a very important reason, to fulfill a vital spiritual mission. Remind them again of their own self-worth - just a*s you* were undoubtedly reminded o*f your*self-worth by your spiritual star brother or star sister long ago.

In doing this meditation, you are bringing the energies full circle — in that you are taking the despair, loneliness and spiritual pain of another star persoi and helping to channel it toward awareness, productivity, and spiritual enlightenment. You are literally creating a complex energy-chain - a chain which will reach around your planet and bring your world one step nearer t global harmony.

In addition to your meditation in this area, we also encourage you to see your own inner harmony level often during this Holiday Season. Remember that the energies of this time of year can be chaotic just as much as they can be joyful. And since you are a high-energy being, it is natural that others who inadvertently try to "draw" on you from time to time — just as plants draw their life-sustaining energy from the sun. But, just like the sun, you must replenish your own energy as well as giving that loving energy to others.

During this time of year, we highly encourage increased meditation as well as nature walks whenever possible. By going out into the quiet parts of the world - such as a field, a lake, an ocean, for example - you can help to protect your own inner peace by "drawing" energy from nature as discussed earlier. By becoming "one" with your planetary fields - even if for a short time - you are becoming a part of the natural energy flow of your Earth, existing in harmony with your planet and all the creatures you share it with.

Finally, we ask you to simply enjoy the goodness of life during this special time of year. Think of what you are even as you think of what you have. Think of what you will do for this world even as you think of what it can/has done for you. And, most of all, think of where you are going as you continue your star mission. The stars of home await you.

May the healing light of God and goodness surround you always,
Tibus.

Comment: Sometimes, it's easy to forget that *we* were once the ones
searching, that *we* were the ones despairing and lonely because we didn't fit in, or just didn't feel like a "part" of this world. And even though we are still not a part of the mundane (Earthly) reality, let us give thanks for the fact that we have learned to be comfortable and happy in the awareness of what we *can* do, what we are here *to* do. Let us give thanks for our *differences,* for it is those differences that set us apart from the Earthly reality, and allow us to perform our destined star tasks.
D.M.T.

TIBUS CHANNELS REGARDING CHRISTMAS, UNIVERSAL LOVE, AND THE STAR PERSON'S ABILITY TO "MANIFEST" GOALS THROUGH CREATIVE VISUALIZATION.

December 1986

As you know, this time on your Earth is indeed a very special time — a time when all living creatures can exist in harmony and peace, a time when all trials and tribulations can be temporarily laid aside in order to share the love which should exist naturally on your lovely blue and green planet.

It has been observed by your star guides such as myself that the holiday season is a time when strangers can become friends, when humanity can be seen at its best. Strangers passing one another on the street will smile, even speak a friendly "Hello"; children become vibrant, the elderly pour out their love, wondering, perhaps, if they will live to see another Christmas, another holiday season, another birthday of their children and grand-children.

It is a time of universal love and brotherhood — a time when even divergent languages are no longer a problem. Voices raise in song, the snow covers parts of the planet in order to protect fragile seedlings which will grow in Spring, and essentially your world renews itself both spiritually and physically.

And yet, it has also been noted that, soon after the New Year begins, this air of festivity and peace lessens; and by February, all remembrance of the holiday season is pretty much past. Perhaps not in the *hearts* of people, but certainly in their attitudes and actions toward one another. It seems peculiar indeed that a species (Man) capable of such love, such affection, such openness during

177

one time of year can become almost completely opposite, showing hostility, jealousy, hatred and so on, once that season is past.

My primary reason for mentioning this is that we want you to know that this need *not* be. Man need not behave one way one minute and a completely opposite way the next minute. In essence, Man is basically a creature of love. He is a *social* animal, with obvious needs for solitude as well. Man needs the company of others of his own kind in order to achieve happiness, to have contentment. And yet, throughout the year, the majority of humanity would appear to seek to drive others like himself away, to isolate himself... perhaps to confirm to his subconscious mind that he is not *worthy* of companionship, even love.

And yet, you *can* make a difference. What would happen if every day were Christmas, or hanukkah, or Valentine's Day? Isn't it possible that many of Man's inborn aggressions would start to lessen if such were the case? And, for that reason, we urge you to live your life as if every day were a day of universal love, brotherhood, a day when all hostilities and aggressions can be laid aside in order to facilitate a more universal goal: that of harmony and peace on Earth.

We understand that you are only one person among approximately 4 billion. And yet, you are a very *important* person, for you are a part of the New Age, you are a more highly evolved spirit, a more advanced soul. And, for that reason, you are existing at all times as an example and a guide to those around you. You are, in essence, a light toward the future, for you show others through your attitudes, actions and spiritual advancement the manner in which the *future* must exist. It is a certainty that, if your world should continue on its present course, there will come a time when all life will be obliteratec — the "good" and the "bad" alike. And so, we urge you to remember that yoi *are* different, you *are* unique, and you are — above all else — a soul advance< beyond your biological and social years.

We also understand that this can be, at times, a burden. And yet, when you embarked on this Earthly life, you chose to carry that weight, to shoulder the responsibility not only for yourself and your loved ones, but for your fellow man as well. We congratulate you on this advanced spiritual decision, and we want you to know that we will support you at all times. When you feel lonely or in doubt, remember to call on your own Special One for guidance, love and assistance. We are with you, my star friend, and we look forward to the day when you will be joined with us in physical reality, too.

Additionally, I would also like to remind you that star people have a very unique ability — the ability to "manifest" certain things into reality. This can be anything from a thought or a concept to a physically real and tangible object. And while that may, on the surface, seem ludicrous or even impossible, we urge you to consider that the mind is, after all, the most powerful human force on your world today.

Do you realize that whenever there is a thought, then that thought becomes reality in some definition? When you think of the love you have for your children or your mate or lover, you have, in essence, *loved* that person. By thinking it, you have activated the process whereby love becomes not only possible but inevitable. Of course, there are varying degrees to which this manifestation process functions. Mainly because there are varying degrees or sincerity within the manifestor, varying degrees of *desire/need* to see that thing/emotion manifested in the first place.

As another example, there are cases in your Earth history whereby theoretically "unreal" things have *become* real because of the desires of people like yourself. Consider space flight. As short a time ago as fifty years, the mere *thought* of spaceflight was considered not only impossible but silly. And yet, because enough people dared to dream, because enough people *wanted* space flight to exist, it did in fact, come into being.

This is no accident. And it can be proven with other examples as well. Consider for a moment the personage of Sherlock Holmes, James Bond, Captain Kirk, Mister Spock or any other seeming "legend" of modern Earth. Even though these characters began as fiction, there has been so much energy applied to them, so many stories written, so many people *needing* them that, in all likelihood, these "fictional characters" have taken on physical flesh and now exist as living beings. In essence, those people who have "dreamed" of these fictional characters have perhaps become spiritual "parents" of actual living entities.

We urge you, if you are interested in this phenomena, to study the works of A.E. Powell — particularly in a book entitled THE ASTRAL BODY. We believe this work will enable you to better understand what we are referring to when we speak of manifestation and creation. And yet, you may wonder *why* this is so important, what bearing or impact it can have on you or your planet. The answer is simple. When star people begin to realize that they *can* manifest thoughts into reality, it will become clear that the thoughts of one person such as yourself *could* mean the difference between destruction and survival on a global scale.

For example, if enough people want peace *enough,* then peace become inevitable. But on the opposite side of the scale, if enough people believe that war is unavoidable, then inevitably war will be fought.

And so, as you can see, it is a matter of mind over reality — a matter of the human mind being able to engineer its own reality through conscious direction of thoughts and desires. More and more, we see evidence that your people are "catching on." The World Moment of Peace is one such example, as are the efforts of certain conservationist groups such as Greenpeace, The Fund For Animals, and so on.

At any rate, please do meditate further on the concept of manifestation and thought-creation. We fully believe that this is *one* answer in your quest for harmony and peace, one answer on your spiritual path toward personal and world-wide fulfillment.

Remember also that we are with you and that you have, in a way, helped to create the atmosphere which allows us to move among you and to share universal views with the people of your planet. Through your efforts, the Earth is changing... and through your continued efforts, it will evolve and grow as your people move into the New Age.

May the healing light of God and goodness surround you always,
Tibus.

Comment: I would just like to add that we are all a part of the Creator —
and perhaps we should realize that, in some small fashion, we have been given the ability to *create,* to change, to mold reality to a more perfect union between Man and his environment. We are all, after all, a small piece of the universal soul, the Universal God-Force, the force of Creation itself. And how we *use* that power is up to us and those like us. D.M.T.

TIBUS CHANNELS REGARDING THE PHENOMENA OF

DEJA VU, AND HOW TIME LOOPS APPLY TO THE STAR
PERSON January 1987

There are several topics I would like to discuss with you during the course of this transmission, and it is my hope that you will give serious thought and meditative awareness to some of the things I am going to tell you. Have you ever wondered about the sensation of deja vu? This is a phenomena which everyone has experienced at some time in their lives, and most people tend to just brush it off or try to explain it in a mundane fashion. And yet, this sensation of "I've done this before" or "I've been here before" is one of the most profound experiences anyone could ever hope to have.

Obviously, you have been driving in a car, perhaps, or involved in a conversation with friends or acquaintances, when suddenly you *know* exactly what is going to happen next. You know what will be around the next corner — in precise detail. Or you know what someone else is going to say — right down to the phrasing and word inflection.

This deja vu experience has existed since Man was advanced enough to understand that he had a mind; and aside from a few attempts by scientists to pass this experience off to "chemical activity in the brain," no one has been able to satisfactorily explain the phenomena. Essentially, it is the belief of your star guides that the deja vu phenomena is basically *proof* that you *have* been in a particular location before, or you *have* had that same conversation at a previous point in your universal life.

More than just evidence to support the reincarnation theories, deja vu is evidence to support the theories contained in quantum mechanics — theories which state that certain "segments" of history/time are circular rather than linear, and that those same segments of history/time are occurring simultaneously on a multitude of dimensional planes.

For example, if we view Time as a location rather than a linear measure of events and history, it becomes possible to understand a little more about how deja vu and other "psychic" events occur. Consider that Time could be a physical entity existing in the space of the Universe — that Time could be a physical *place,* another "world" just as the Earth, the moon, Venus, Mars and the other planets are other worlds. It is simply that the world of Time is far more complex and more difficult to see than these other physical places.

And yet, I transmit to you now that Time is no less "real" than the Earth, the moon or the stars. And for that reason, Time becomes a phenomena to be reckoned with - a force with which all living things much contend if they are to grow and evolve on the Cosmic Evolutionary Scale.

I use the example of deja vu to highlight the fact that there are "loops" in time as well — moments when Time becomes temporarily out of synch with itself — just as earthquakes, volcanic eruptions and even violent storms are moments when the physical Earth becomes out of synch with itself. The sensation of deja vu is one which star people such as yourself should explore fully - for when you begin to comprehend the nature of deja vu more fully, it will become possible for you to more fully understand the concept of actual *time travel.* Essentially, we star guides are as much from your future as we are from the stars — and it is our strong impression and belief that you can begin to travel the galaxy in your own lifetime — partially through a more thorough understanding of time loops.

When you experience deja vu, what is your reaction? Do you get chills or try to pretend "it isn't happening"? Do you try to analyze it while it is happening? Or do you find it a "good" feeling? Your own reaction to this phenomena is of great importance — for it could give you valuable "clues" as to where you are *going* in your own future.

If, for example, deja vu leaves you with a feeling of uneasiness or distress, it is possible that your "temporary future" (that future which will exist if you continue on your present course) is not very good. If deja vu leaves with you a sensation of wonder or great joy or elation, then your "temporary future" is undoubtedly "in line" with your personal Cosmic Destiny (in other words, you are undoubtedly on the right path). I mention these things mainly to illustrate the potential for you to change the future in what is usually a split second! If, for example, you experience the deja vu phenomena and your reaction is a "negative" one, what you must realize is that this is a crossroads in time — a moment when all of collective reality is singling you out and offering you an opportunity to "change" something in your own future.

In other words, the time loop theory states that your future has many possible paths and, depending on which of those paths you choose, your future will be different. Thus, when you experience a negative reaction to the deja vu phenomena, you should "go with it" for as long as the experience will last. Open yourself to the experience and see how far/long the sensations will last. *Don't start analyzing the moment you realize it's happening*; instead, let your mind "give in" to the experience and follow it through to its conclusion.

Then, when the sensations stop and you are once again in "real time," take a good look at your life and what you are doing and where you are headed in your "temporary future." Are you satisfied in your job? Are you enjoyingyour family relationships? Are you satisfied with your level of spiritual growth and development? In short, what needs changing in your life?

Of course, the deja vu experience is only one "indicator" of your temporary future, and you will need to take many factors into account before making any major decisions which will change your entire life. And yet, by examining the deja vu sensations, it is our feeling that you will get a much clearer picture of where your life may be taking you.

Additionally, consider the time loop theory in more detail. Essentially, a loop in time is something which occurs for a variety of reasons. For example, time travellers must be very cautious to avoid getting "caught" in a time loop - i.e., time travellers must exercise caution to guard against travelling back in time and then returning to their "future" (actually their own "natural" time) before they left.

For example, consider what could happen if you travelled back in time. Let's say you started your journey at 8:00 A.M. on January 1,1987, and that you were travelling back in time to 8:00 A.M. on January 1,1800. When you arrive in the year 1800, you could spend weeks or even years without any real "effect" on you or on your own "natural time" (1987). *But,* when you are ready to return to your natural time, what would happen if you miscalculated and returned home at 7:59 A.M., January 1,1987. Essentially, if this should occur, you would become caught in a time loop — for obviously at 7:59 A.M. on January 1, 1987, you were just preparing to *depart* on your journey.

Thus, the deja vu experience could also be indicative of the fate of many time travellers — perhaps time travellers with whom you have come into contact. In other words, if you were to meet a time traveller who had become trapped in the loop, it stands to reason that *you* would become a *part* of his/ her loop. In other words, you would "feel" the loop bending back on itself when you essentially "passed yourself" on the journey forward or backwards in time. One of the great questions of time travel concerns whether or not a person could travel back in time ten years and talk to his/her former self - him/herself as he/she was ten years in the past. Obviously, if this could be done, it would enable people to avoid serious mistakes they had made on their life's journey, and would subsequently enable them to make intelligent choices based on *future* knowledge.

We star guides feel that further investigation and meditation on the deja vu and time loop theory would prove very valuable to you for a variety of reasons. We encourage you to give thought and to increase your awareness on this subject; for it is my impression that this information will be important to you in the very near future.

Most of all, we encourage you to remember that Time is an entity — a physical, living thing, just as are all the other creatures of the galaxy. And, for that reason, Time can be reckoned with, can become a friend rather than an unseen foe. And, of course, when Time becomes a friend, the knowledge to be gained and the range of possible experiences will increase geometrically.

Also, remember that your own Special One is always there to guide and help you further, and that by applying the full force of your energy toward your Special One, you will always receive the guidance you are seeking.

May the healing light of God and goodness surround you always,
Tibus.

Comment: I would just like to comment that time loops are almost certainly an established fact for the star person such as yourself. Because of the nature of your earthly mission, it stands to reason that you have had contact with many time travellers — either in the physical realm or in the astral realms. So, the next time you experience the deja vu phenomena, I encourage you to examine the reaction it produces within you, and to further examine your life and mission here, too.

If you have a positive reaction to the experience, then you are undoubtedly "on the right path." If you have a more typically "negative" reaction, perhaps you should, as Tibus suggested, examine your life's path to see what changes might be necessary to "set things straight" in your life. D.M.T.

TIBUS CHANNELS ON THE CONCEPTS OF FREEDOM AND IMPRISONMENT, AND OFFERS HELPFUL GUIDELINES FOR PERSONAL MEDITATION

February 1987

Inner well-being is the first step toward universal oneness — a fact which even the most spiritually and/or psychically aware individuals tend to over look from time to time.

Very often, those of your world spend their days in search of wealth or social status, and their evenings are spent in pursuit of relationships, or attempting to recover from the pressures which have mounted and grown throughout the day. And, as the star person such as yourself can surely recognize, this "vicious circle" is difficult if not often impossible to "break." For that reason, it is essential that you remember to *always* turn inward for your own sense of peace and well being — that you establish a safe "home base" within your own heart and mind where you can retreat during times of turmoil or stress.

We star guides realize that the word "meditation" has come to be a vastly overused term - one which means many things to many different people. However, when we speak of meditation, we are referring to the inner search ing, to the state of mind wherein the star person can find answers, and can ask questions of himself or even of his own Special One.

To clarify, meditation ideally should be a state of *being* as much as it is a state of mind. By this, we mean simply that, when you meditate, you should ideally be "travelling" to an inner sanctuary which exists within the soul of every living creature. This sanctuary is not one which will make itself known to you without meditation, nor is it a "place" where someone should "run" to escape worldly or personal problems. Rather, this inner sanctuary is a place of comfort and security, much like churches represent sanctuary to some, or as temples or synagogues represent sanctuary to others.When you meditate, strive to actually "see" this inner sanctuary as a physically real place to which only you have the key. It may appear to you as a garden with beautiful flowers, very secluded and walled off from the outside world. Or it may appear as a vast expanse of the desert,

185

open and all- encompassing for as far as the eye can see; or a seashore with warm breezes, or a forest with tall trees and filtered sun creating shadows on the ground.

However your inner sanctuary appears to you really isn't important in the long run. What *is* important is that you develop a strong sense of that *place,* allowing it to manifest and become very "real" in your mind -- as real and alive as some place you have visited, for example. Thus, when you *do* meditate, you will always be drawn to this place, and will be able to fall immediately into a sense of "familiarity" which will deliver your mind into an instant state of peace and serenity.

I feel that these things bear mention for several reasons, not the least of which is that many people simply do not know or use the proper techniques of meditation. There is, as you know, more to meditation than simply "thinking." In fact, meditation is the art of *not* thinking - the ability to let your conscious mind rest and allow your subconscious (or Super Consciousness) to explore a variety of concepts and sensations which are simply not possible so long as the conscious (or Mundane/Earthly) mind is in control.

Additionally, I feel this information on meditation is going to be very valuable to you over the weeks and months ahead; for it is my impression that you are entering a period in your life which will bring about many changes. And in order to make sound decisions, you are going to need this inner sanctuary which I have described to you above. You will need a "place" to retreat to — a place where answers can be sought and discovered, a place where your soul can experience the ultimate freedom despite the pressures and mental "prisons" imposed on you by the Earthly/Mundane reality.

Which brings me to the main point of this reading — the concept of prisons or imprisonment, or the loss of personal freedom. This loss of freedom could come in any form — from a political/global situation to a more personal and less widespread phenomena.

And, what *is* freedom? Is it simply the ability to say and do certain things without fear of legal repercussions? Or is it the inherent right of individuals to live in a certain manner and carry on their lives as they see fit? Or, more precisely, is freedom simply the right to *live?*

Additionally, what is imprisonment? Is it what happens when freedom is taken away in one manner or another? Or is imprisonment something which exists solely in the mind of an individual at any given time?

For example, it is possible to walk through your Earthly society as a legally "free" individual, living your life as you see fit, doing the things you please. And yet, are you ever *really* free? Can you *really* do those things your soul longs to do, or are you prevented from doing this by restraints and/or fears which have been placed upon you by others in your society?

At any rate, it is important to realize that freedom and imprisonment will mean something different to almost everyone. Ideally, the people of your Earth should be free to pursue their happiness in *whatever* unharmful manner they choose. And yet, because of government restraints and technological "impossibilities," such is not the case. For the most part, you are a "prisoner" of your world — and for that reason, a certain "freedom" has been denied to you.

I transmit to you at this time that the technology currently exists on your planet which could take men and women to the stars — not only to the nearest planets such as Mars, Venus or even Pluto -- but to the stars themselves. And yet, this technology is withheld from the public because of governmental fears and petty jealousies. Most Earth governments don't *want* their people going to the stars or even having the possibility of going to the stars. For the most part, governments are designed to rule rather than to lead; and as you have discerned through your own meditations and studies, there is a vast difference between a leader and a ruler.

Also, governments are afraid of losing their authority and power should Mankind ever begin to venture forth to the stars - for how would these petty governments keep track of vast numbers of people? How would they "control" millions of people living on thousands of different worlds? And, ultimately, why is control so important to these individuals? Why must governments seek to subjugate and dictate rather than to promote creativity and support dreams?

In essence, this need to control goes back to Man's earliest days on the Earth — when it was perhaps necessary to "control" certain elements in order to insure survival. For example, in the days of the "cave man," it was perhaps necessary to control dangerous animals — and yet, to this day, we see hunters killing helpless creatures for the sake of "sport." We see fishermen slaughtering whales and dolphins because it is easier to kill rather than to utilize existing technology to prevent or even dramatically reduce the numbers of these needless killings.

In essence, Man's craving for power is a vestigial remnant of his earliest days on this planet. Many have overcome the need to kill in order to eat, becoming vegetarians. Many have overcome the desire to subjugate and control others. Many have learned that Man was put here to *share* his world with the animals rather than to rule or control them. And yet, for every person who *has* learned this valuable lesson, there are thousands more who have not. And until that lesson can be learned by a vast *majority* rather than a struggling minority, your Earth will remain in the control of "barbarians" — individuals who are living down to their lowest potential rather than living up to their highest possibilities.

Again, we encourage you to remember that freedom and imprisonment are as much abstract concepts as they are concrete realities. At any time, you have the ability to retreat into your inner sanctuary of meditation. But we urge you to bring that serenity *back* with you when you return to the mundane/ Earthy reality. In doing so, you will essentially be projecting freedom (abstract or real) to those around you. You will basically be creating a "pocket" of ultimate freedom which will eventually begin to spread. As the people of your planet learn more about their nature, and as they learn to overcome the "negative" aspects of human nature, they will begin taking giant steps toward *ultimate* freedom rather than allowing themselves to be content with "surface" (Earthly) freedoms.

I urge you to meditate on the concept of freedom and imprisonment over the next few weeks, and to keep a diary of the conclusions you reach through this inner searching. Be particularly aware of your "surroundings" during your meditation, and notice how those surroundings may change subtly on a daily or weekly basis. All these things are indicative of your own spiritual growth and development, and of how you are helping to shape your planet. By creating and enjoying your *own* ultimate freedom through meditation, you will inevitably "spread" that freedom — and the *need* for that freedom — to others. And, of course, recognizing the need for something is the first step toward realizing it in a physical and lasting way.

May the healing light of God and goodness surround you

always,
Tibus

Comment As you pursue the concepts and ideas of freedom, remember that your "ultimate freedom" as Tibus calls it is basically whatever you conceive it to be. Perhaps your ultimate freedom would be travelling to the stars. Or perhaps your ultimate freedom would be that of being able to live in a place without having the constant threat of new housing projects destroying the environment. Perhaps your ultimate freedom is gaining some spiritual ability, such as the ability to astrally project, or the ability to communicate more clearly with your own Special One.

Whatever your ultimate freedom may be, both Tibus and I encourage you to seek it always, to find it in the private sanctuary of your meditations, and to ultimately superimpose that freedom on the real world - thereby making it a reality which you can live as well as dream.

D.M.T.

16

THE STAR NETWORK
DIANE TESSMAN, P.P., D.L.
P.O. BOX 352 Ansgar, Iowa 50472

And so, dear friends, we all await the Transformation in our own unique ways. However, we also await the Transformation together.

We are being drawn closer and closer together with each passing day. The Star Network is being formed in rapid, thrilling, and spectacular fashion. "Intersect points" are lighting up on a cosmic network all over planet Earth. The Network is coming together in final preparation for the difficult times at hand and ahead.

Tibus channels to me that all we have to define the dimension around us is our mind/soul; in fact, your mind/soul has created the world around you to a very large degree! It can just as easily create a new and shining reality for Our Space Brothers know that mind/soul is ALL and that your soul is a segment of the Great Cosmic Soul! God can be brought into your life via a Divine Energy Frequency (much like tuning into a radio station!) and many blessings can be yours.

With many, many people on the positive frequency, Tibus assures me there is also a chance that the violence of the catastrophes can be much-lessened or even eliminated so that the human race will be able to move into the magnificent transformation - a higher level of human consciousness without the tragedy and upheaval which is expected.

We must also stand ready for overt contact with the higher realms of consciousness, both extraterrestrial and with humans from a risen future (time travelers). You must be able to tell others not to be afraid as face to face contact is made and as The Change (Shift) begins to take place. Because you know your own heart, mind, and soul...and know your own beautiful place in the Divine Cosmos, you will stand a better chance of surviving global disasters and changes...and you can help others who do not have this Cosmic Wisdom and Insight.

It is of urgent importance that we do connect, seek each other out, embrace and support each other. The preparations for the Change Point are mapped out in specific stages. These stages are much like the ones which Dr. Sprinkle mapped at the beginning of the book:

Anxiety, Analysis, Awareness,Acceptance, Acknowledgement, Assessment, and Action.

We are now at the final stage, the Action Stage! We must be strong and aware now and turn our negative energies to Divine Positive Energy. We must take action to make our own lives better as well as the life of Planet Earth better (as Jesus said, "Peace on Earth, Good Will Toward Men.")

There is a great aloneness among us and a great need to make contact, to touch, to reach out to others like ourselves. Yet, we do not know how to go about it, do not know what to do next. Many, many people have joined THE STAR NETWORK HEARTLINE and have found that answer and many more! I hope you will, too! Please feel free to contact me. You can reach me either through postal mail or through info@earthchangepredictions.com

OTHER BOOKS BY DIANE TESSMAN

UFO AGENDA
http://www.amazon.com/The-UFO-Agenda-Diane-Tessman-ebook/dp/B00DUEPPJ4

SEVEN RAYS OF THE HEALING MILLENIUM
http://www.amazon.com/Seven-Healing-Millennium-Diane-Tessman/dp/0938294741

THE GOD CLOUD AND OTHER EARTH CHANGES REVELATIONS

EARTH CHANGES BIBLE

Made in the USA
Las Vegas, NV
11 February 2022